# THE COASTAL ALMANAC

A Series of Books in Geology

Editor: *Allan Cox*

# THE COASTAL ALMANAC

For 1980 — The Year of the Coast

by

*Paul L. Ringold*

and

*John Clark*

The Conservation Foundation
Washington, D.C.

W. H. Freeman and Company
*San Francisco*

This document was prepared especially for "1980—The Year of the Coast" by The Conservation Foundation, Washington, D.C., in cooperation with The Coastal Alliance, Washington, D.C.

Cover: The Chesapeake Bay to New York City from outer space. (Photograph courtesy of NASA)

**Library of Congress Cataloging in Publication Data**

Ringold, Paul L
   The coastal almanac for 1980—The Year of the Coast.

   (A Series of books in geology)
   Bibliography: p.
   Includes index.
   1.  Coasts—United States.   2.   Coastal zone management—
United States.   I.   Clark, John R., 1927–
joint author.   II.   Title.
GB460.A2R56        333.91'7'0973        80-22501
ISBN 0-7167-1285-7
ISBN 0-7167-1286-5 (pbk.)

Printed in the United States of America

9  8  7  6  5  4  3  2  1

**The Conservation Foundation**
1717 Massachusetts Avenue, N.W., Washington, D.C. 20036
Telephone (202)797-4300  Cable CONSERVIT

**The Conservation Foundation** (1717 Massachusetts Avenue, N.W., Washington, D.C. 20036) is a nonprofit research and communication organization dedicated to encouraging human conduct to sustain and enrich life on earth. Since its founding in 1948, it has attempted to provide intellectual leadership in the cause of wise management of the earth's resources.

Frontispiece. Thunder Hole. Arcadia National Park, Maine.
(Photograph by Frank Givens, National Park Service)

"NATURE TO BE COMMANDED MUST BE OBEYED"

Francis Bacon
1620

# TABLE OF CONTENTS

# FOREWORD

The celebration of 1980 as the Year of the Coast provided us the opportunity to satisfy a long standing ambition; to produce an almanac of basic information about coastal resources. The collaboration of our senior ecologist, John Clark, with marine ecologist, Paul L. Ringold, of The Johns Hopkins University, has resulted in a compilation that I believe will be of great benefit to government admnistrators, conservationists, developers, students and communicators.

I see the Coastal Almanac as an important contribution to the conservation cause of this country as we address ourselves to the changing directions of the 1980's. I strongly sense that the new decade will lead the conservation community to return to its historical concern about resources and to reassert the central role of resource conservation to the long-term health of society. Never before has resource conservation been so essential to the national well-being. Never before has there been a stronger need to conserve our coastal resources.

Certainly, a more concerted effort is needed if we hope to maintain the present level of our commercial fisheries. The majority of commercial fishing takes place close to the continental shelf or in shallow coastal bays. Many of the fish that do live in the ocean, such as salmon and striped bass, have critical breeding links to coastal estuaries or rivers. In these nursery areas, the young stages are especially vulnerable to pollution and habitat alteration. Therefore, the water quality and general condition of the coastal environment must be maintained in good condition.

Shellfisheries are particularly vulnerable to pollution. Because shellfish can take up human pathogens from sewage in the water -- hepatitis, dysentery, and others -- their catch in polluted waters is prohibited by state and federal health laws. While many shellfish areas are open and prospering at present, nearly 4 million acres are closed to shellfishing.

Sportfishing, recreational boating, camping and nature study are important recreational diversions that our coastal resources offer, but the foremost recreational resource is the beach itself.  However, private developments along the coastline are locking off thousands of miles of shoreline.

Coastal sprawl is probably the leading cause of diminishing access to beaches and waters.  Large-scale condominium projects and private home development have caused heavy demand for bridges and causeways to open up new lands and have created a need for sewers and other capital items to service new communities.  Carelessly planned, intense private use of land closes out the public and endangers coastal resources.  Reserving beaches for the public has often been ignored or obstructed by local governments.

Sprawl also encourages bulkheading, groins, and jetties that erode the beach because of a complex of physical reactions of waves to hard structures.  The problem is greatly exacerbated by the slow and relentless rise of sea level throughout the world.  Erosion due to reckless development combined with natural forces is a serious and costly national problem.

These and many other problems must receive more concerted conservation attention in the 1980's than ever before.  Federal programs, such as the Coastal Zone Management program of the Department of Commerce, cannot do it all.  Local governments and their constitutents will have to collaborate far more willingly with state and federal agencies to achieve coastal conservation goals.  It is to aid in the widened conservation dialog that is certain to occupy the 1980's that this almanac is dedicated.  I believe it will be a significant contribution.

William K. Reilly
President, The Conservation Foundation
June, 1980

# PREFACE

This almanac was prepared as a central reference for people involved with use and conservation of the coastal resources of the continental United States and the effects of natural hazards. The coast has been brought to public attention as never before by official celebration of 1980 as the "Year of the Coast." We believe that the expanded dialog on coastal issues will be enhanced by a common source of statistical information. We hope that ecologists, developers, students, administrators, engineers, civic activists, scientists, planners, and writers will all benefit from this compilation.

The coast of America is more than harbors and beaches. It is an interacting natural system of water, land, bays, wetlands, tideflats, birds, fishes, and vistas. Man's actions intermingle with nature's system along the coasts with results that are sometimes synergistic and often antagonistic. Nature, as always, sets the stage upon which man operates.

Just as the value of the coast lies in the diversity of its resources, the extensive conflicts over uses and conservation of resources arise from the great variety of uses of the coast. Coastal users compete for space along the shoreline. Neither a residential development nor a berth for cargo ships can share the same location along the water's edge. Other forms of competition in the coast are less obvious. A filled wetland can no longer provide habitat or food for wildlife or fishes. Oil spread on a beach reduces many of the qualities that we value in a beach. Heavy metals, human sewage, and other effluents can reduce the value of fisheries, and the desirability of recreation in our waters. Decisions about how to resolve these conflicts among the users of the coast should be made carefully and on the basis of fact. It is our hope that this book will contribute many of the facts needed in the decision process.

We expect that the reader will use this book as a reference for general purposes and as a beginning point for deeper examination of subjects. In either case the reader should be critical of the information presented here and carefully examine its sources.

Many people have played an important role in the preparation of this book. We thank Ruth Ann Hill for drafting the original figures, and for her assistance in constructing several of the tables. Laura O'Sullivan capably shepherded the book throughout its development. Tony Brown deserves much praise for his cheerful willingness in typing difficult copy. The senior author (Ringold) thanks "DJ" for her patience -- the time spent writing this book was otherwise hers.

We are grateful to Terry Davies, Vice President of The Conservation Foundation, who facilitated the creation of the almanac in many ways, and to John Staples of W. H. Freeman and Company, whose foresight and enthusiasm led to its publication. Dallas Miner and Catherine Morrison of the federal office of Coastal Zone Management deserve credit for providing support for the almanac project at a critical time. The support of the Jessie Smith Noyes Foundation for intern assistance is also greatly appreciated. We thank Bob Peoples, and John Nagy for making their unpublished data available to us.

This book has benefited from the advice of dozens of colleagues who often painstakingly reviewed every digit of our tables. Their efforts are deeply appreciated. However, whatever residual errors remain are our responsibility.


June, 1980                                Paul L. Ringold
                                          John Clark

# INTRODUCTION

The information selected for presentation in this almanac was selected on the basis of relevance to resource issues, the quality of data, and economy in production of the document. We have selected data that are nationwide or regional in scope and, to the extent feasible, available by individual states. We have selected data that are recent in time, collected by known and uniform standards, and that related to natural resources. We excluded Alaska, usually, because it is less well known, studied, and catalogued, and because it is unique in so many ways. We excluded Hawaii, usually, because it also is unique in many ways. We also excluded the Great Lakes in order to focus on the ocean coast, although it is popular these days to talk of the great lakes as part of the nation's "coastal zone".

We have organized the data tables by natural resource categories and by the categories of use of the resources. Thus, information on recreational fish catches appears in a fisheries resource category while data on cash expenditures and days spent fishing appears in a use category with other recreational information.

The information that we present is derived largely from existing publications. In some cases, we have copied material directly from original sources; distilling the most important facts. In other cases (e.g., Tables 32d, 36, 38, and 45c) we have reorganized available information and presented it in new formats to reveal fresh insights. In some instances, we have taken raw information and analyzed it by our own methods (e.g., Tables 8, 9, 20, 21, 23, and 30).

While the federal government collects a great many facts, many of them are unavailable in a form that relates specifically or comprehensively to the coastal zone. For example, the government provides insurance to homeowners in flood prone areas but detailed information is not available about the extent and type of coastal investment, the proportion of policies in high hazard zones, the extent of land use controls provided by local government for resource protection, and so forth. Similarly, the federal

1

government has a large investment in wetlands protection but has not produced a recent national inventory of wetland types and the extent of past losses.

On the positive side, we are able to use some of the massive amount of general statistical data which, though not specifically oriented to the coast, can be used for coastal purposes where available on a county-by-county basis. In order to make use of this information, we have compiled a list of coastal counties which we have designated as being truly coastal in character. The information on energy, agriculture, employment, and population in the coast is all based on this county list.

Each table, or set of tables is preceded by interpretative comments which may briefly state the significance of the data and select a few highlights to bring to the reader's attention. Where necessary, we have added caveats about potential problems and limitations of the data, or we have described the origins of the data.

# I  SHOREFRONT

The coast consists of uplands and wetlands adjacent to and interacting with oceans and estuarine waters, as well as whatever freshwater may be a part of it.  In contrast to this broad ill-defined band, or zone, the shorefront is itself the edge where land and water meet. It is the line we cross going from one realm to the other.

We provide in this section some of the fundamental characteristics describing this place -- how big it is, who owns it, what do we do with it, how we have tried to protect it.  Barrier islands are given considerable attention in this section, because they are so heavily influenced by the forces of the sea -- storms, tides, currents, and winds--and are therefore often poorly suited for occupancy.

# 1. SHORELINE LENGTH

The length of the shoreline--the boundary between the land and the sea or its estuaries--provides the basic description of the coast.  Several measures of the length of the shoreline have been developed  for a variety of uses. The differing measures reflect different amounts of shoreline detail.  The Department of Commerce has devised two measures: 1) the "General Shoreline" which includes only those sounds and bays that have entrances wider than 30 miles, and then only to the point where they narrow to this distance.  (Thus, this measure does not include the shoreline of the Chesapeake or San Francisco Bays, for example), and 2) the "Tidal Shoreline" which includes the shores of tidal waters to the head of tidewater, or to a point where tidal waters narrow to a width of 100 feet.  The U.S. Army Corps of Engineers has devised a separate measure: the "National Shoreline" which also goes to the head of tidewater.

Table 1. LENGTH OF THE UNITED STATES SHORELINE.

| | General Coastline[1] | Tidal Shoreline[1] | National Shoreline[2] |
|---|---|---|---|
| United States | 13,443 | 91,154 | 80,577 |
| Coterminous only | 4,993 | 53,677 | 32,344 |
| Atlantic | 2,069 | 28,673 | 18,691 |
| Gulf of Mexico | 1,631 | 17,141 | 8,989 |
| Pacific | 7,623 | 40,298 | 52,897 |
| Artic | 1,060 | 2,521 | --- |
| Maine | 228 | 3,478 | 2,500 |
| New Hampshire | 13 | 131 | 40 |
| Massachusetts | 192 | 1,519 | 1,200 |
| Rhode Island | 40 | 384 | 340 |
| Connecticut | --- | 618 | 270 |
| New York | 127 | 1,850 | 638 |
| New Jersey | 130 | 1,792 | 469 |
| Pennsylvania | --- | 89 | --- |
| Delaware | 28 | 381 | 226 |
| Maryland | 31 | 3,190 | 1,939 |
| Virginia | 112 | 3,315 | 993 |
| North Carolina | 301 | 3,375 | 3,661 |
| South Carolina | 187 | 2,876 | 3,063 |
| Georgia | 100 | 2,344 | 204 |
| Florida (Atlantic only) | 580 | 3,331 | 2,316 |
| Florida (Gulf only) | 770 | 5,095 | 3,949 |
| Florida (Atlantic and Gulf) | 1,350 | 8,426 | 6,265 |
| Alabama | 53 | 607 | 352 |
| Mississippi | 44 | 359 | 247 |
| Louisiana | 397 | 7,721 | 1,943 |
| Texas | 367 | 3,359 | 2,498 |
| California | 840 | 3,427 | 1,827 |
| Oregon | 296 | 1,410 | 500 |
| Washington | 157 | 3,026 | 2,337 |
| Alaska (Pacific only) | 5,580 | 31,383 | --- |
| Alaska (Artic only) | 1,060 | 2,521 | --- |
| Alaska (Pacific and Artic) | 6,640 | 33,904 | 47,300 |
| Hawaii | 750 | 1,052 | 930 |

Sources: [1]U.S. Department of Commerce, NOAA. 1975. The Coastline of the United States; [2]U.S. Army Corps of Engineers. 1971. The National Shoreline Study.

# 2. SHORELINE OWNERSHIP

The ownership of the shoreline is a major factor in determining who has access from land to sea. This table summarizes the ownership of the shoreline shoreward of <u>Mean High Water</u>, most of which is privately owned (in the majority of states, the land seaward of Mean High Water is public property). Public ownership landward of Mean High water is at a minimum in the North Atlantic region (13%), and at a maximum in the South Atlantic region (56%). Note: "Non-federal public" ownership is land owned by the states, counties or other non-federal public entity.

Table 2. OWNERSHIP OF THE SHORELINE BY STATE.

| State or Region | Federal Miles | % | Non-Federal Public Miles | % | Private Miles | % |
|---|---|---|---|---|---|---|
| Maine | 20 | * | 60 | 2 | 2420 | 97 |
| New Hampshire | 2 | 5 | 10 | 25 | 28 | 70 |
| Massachusetts | 90 | 8 | 175 | 15 | 935 | 78 |
| Rhode Island | 10 | 3 | 50 | 15 | 280 | 82 |
| Connecticut | 5 | 2 | 50 | 19 | 215 | 80 |
| New York | 34 | 5 | 202 | 32 | 402 | 63 |
| New Jersey | 67 | 14 | 130 | 28 | 272 | 58 |
| Delaware | 12 | 5 | 46 | 20 | 168 | 74 |
| Maryland | 225 | 12 | 35 | 2 | 1679 | 87 |
| Virginia | 109 | 11 | 115 | 12 | 769 | 77 |
| North Carolina[1] | 573 | 16 | 59 | 2 | 1038 | 28 |
| South Carolina[1] | 435 | 14 | 1452 | 47 | 832 | 27 |
| Georgia | 29 | 14 | 23 | 11 | 153 | 75 |
| Florida[1] | 689 | 11 | 277 | 4 | 5203 | 83 |
| Florida (Atlantic)[1] | 159 | 7 | 87 | 4 | 2028 | 88 |
| Florida (Gulf)[1] | 530 | 13 | 190 | 5 | 3175 | 80 |
| Alabama | 2 | * | 13 | 4 | 337 | 96 |
| Mississippi | 33 | 13 | 43 | 17 | 171 | 69 |
| Louisiana | 246 | 13 | 332 | 17 | 1366 | 70 |
| Texas | 388 | 16 | 55 | 2 | 2055 | 82 |
| California | 411 | 22 | 357 | 20 | 1057 | 58 |
| Oregon | 83 | 17 | 158 | 32 | 238 | 48 |
| Washington | 155 | 7 | 107 | 5 | 2075 | 89 |
| TOTAL[1] | 3618 | 11 | 3749 | 12 | 21693 | 67 |
| | | | | | | |
| Maine to Virginia | 574 | 7 | 873 | 11 | 7168 | 87 |
| North Carolina to Atlantic Florida[1] | 1196 | 13 | 1621 | 18 | 4051 | 44 |
| Gulf Florida to Texas | 1199 | 13 | 633 | 7 | 7104 | 79 |
| Pacific | 649 | 14 | 622 | 13 | 3370 | 72 |

[1] Some shoreline of uncertain ownership
* Less than 1%
Source: U.S. Army Corps of Engineers, 1971. <u>The National Shoreline Study</u>.

# 3. SHORELINE USES

How has the shoreline been portioned among major uses?  This table provides the answer by four, broad categories.  Public recreational shoreline -- including public parks, boat launch ramps and moorage facilities for recreation -- has the smallest slice.  Private recreational shoreline -- including similar facilities for private use -- is next.  Non-recreational shoreline -- including shoreline developed for nonrecreational activities, such as industries, residences, and harbors -- is second to largest.  Undeveloped shoreline with no facilities -- including considerable recreational opportunity for those who would rough it -- has the largest slice.

Table 3.   THE USES OF THE SHORELINE BY STATE.

| State or Region | Public Recreation Miles | % | Private Recreation Miles | % | Nonrecreational Developed Miles | % | Undeveloped Miles | % |
|---|---|---|---|---|---|---|---|---|
| Maine | 13 | * | 967 | 39 | 260 | 10 | 1260 | 50 |
| New Hampshire | 8 | 20 | 30 | 75 | 2 | 5 | 0 | 0 |
| Massachusetts | 235 | 20 | 800 | 67 | 85 | 7 | 80 | 7 |
| Rhode Island | 50 | 15 | 270 | 79 | 20 | 6 | 0 | 0 |
| Connecticut | 30 | 11 | 225 | 83 | 15 | 6 | 0 | 0 |
| New York | 210 | 33 | 70 | 11 | 250 | 39 | 108 | 17 |
| New Jersey | 290 | 62 | 35 | 7 | 12 | 3 | 132 | 28 |
| Delaware | 33 | 15 | 34 | 15 | 3 | 1 | 156 | 69 |
| Maryland | 105 | 5 | 111 | 6 | 1623 | 84 | 100 | 5 |
| Virginia | 50 | 5 | 56 | 6 | 155 | 16 | 732 | 74 |
| North Carolina | 98 | 3 | 321 | 9 | 239 | 7 | 3003 | 82 |
| South Carolina | 84 | 3 | 50 | 2 | 580 | 19 | 2349 | 77 |
| Georgia | 16 | 8 | 5 | 3 | 0 | 0 | 183 | 89 |
| Florida | 386 | 6 | 763 | 12 | 1445 | 23 | 3672 | 59 |
| Alabama | 32 | 9 | 210 | 60 | 5 | 1 | 105 | 30 |
| Mississippi | 31 | 13 | 106 | 43 | 10 | 4 | 101 | 41 |
| Louisiana | 18 | * | 28 | 1 | 46 | 2 | 1851 | 95 |
| Texas | 386 | 15 | 160 | 6 | 107 | 4 | 1845 | 74 |
| California | 432 | 24 | 178 | 10 | 228 | 12 | 989 | 54 |
| Oregon | 205 | 41 | 81 | 16 | 110 | 22 | 104 | 21 |
| Washington | 147 | 6 | 40 | 2 | 77 | 3 | 2073 | 89 |
| TOTAL | 2859 | 9 | 4542 | 14 | 5272 | 17 | 18843 | 60 |
| | | | | | | | | |
| Maine to Virginia | 1024 | 12 | 2598 | 30 | 2425 | 28 | 2568 | 30 |
| North Carolina to Texas | 1051 | 6 | 1645 | 9 | 2432 | 13 | 13109 | 72 |
| Pacific | 784 | 17 | 299 | 6 | 415 | 20 | 3166 | 68 |

* Less than 1%
Source:  U.S. Army Corps of Engineers, 1971.  The National Shoreline Study.

# 4. BEACH LENGTH

Sunbathing is the core of a coastal vacation. The states are blessed with varying amounts of beaches -- from 2 to 79% of their total shoreline. The Pacific coast has the highest percentage of shoreline as beaches (55%), but states on other coasts may also have extensive beaches.

The definition of a beach in the National Shoreline Study (from which this information is taken) is somewhat variable. Most Corps Districts define a beach as an area with sand between high and low tide, but one District (Alaska) calls it an area of unconsolidated material between the low and extreme high waterlines.

Table 4. LENGTH OF BEACH BY STATE.

| State | Miles of Beach | Pct. of National Shoreline in Beaches | State or Region | Miles of Beach | Pct. of National Shoreline in Beaches |
|---|---|---|---|---|---|
| Maine | 60 | 2 | Alabama | 227 | 65 |
| New Hampshire | 25 | 63 | Mississippi | 97 | 39 |
| Massachusetts | 940 | 78 | Louisiana | 835 | 43 |
| Rhode Island | 185 | 54 | Texas | 377 | 15 |
| Connecticut | 145 | 54 | California | 412 | 23 |
| New York | 331 | 52 | Oregon | 300 | 60 |
| New Jersey | 215 | 46 | Washington | 1847 | 79 |
| Delaware | 76 | 34 | TOTAL | 10983 | 30 |
| Maryland | 46 | 2 | | | |
| Virginia | 294 | 30 | Maine to Virginia | 2320 | 27 |
| North Carolina | 1269 | 35 | North Carolina to | | |
| South Carolina | 196 | 6 | Atlantic Florida | 3600 | 25 |
| Georgia | 102 | 50 | Florida Gulf to | | |
| Florida Atlantic | 390 | 15 | Texas | 2504 | 29 |
| Florida Gulf | 968 | 26 | Pacific | 2559 | 55 |

[1] See Table 1 for "National Shoreline" lengths by State.
Source: U.S. Army Corps of Engineers. 1971. The National Shoreline Study.

# 5. SHORELINE EROSION

Nature continually shapes the coastline. It tears sediments away from one place (erosion), and leaves them in another (deposition). Erosion and deposition may operate in the same place but during different seasons (see below). Many areas have undergone net erosion loss in recent years. Nationwide, almost half of our shores are eroding. The North Atlantic states have the highest percentage of erosion, while the South Atlantic states have the lowest. New York is the state with the highest percentage of eroding shoreline (100%), and Washington State has the lowest percentage of eroding shoreline (4%).

Erosion is a natural hazard and presents a problem for the owners and users of many shoreline developments and facilities. In this table, there are two classes of erosion. The first is critical, and the second is noncritical. An area experiencing one or the other is significantly eroding. Critical erosion is erosion which "presents a serious problem because the rate of erosion considered in conjunction with economic, industrial, recreational, agricultural, navigational, demographic, ecological, and other relevant factors indicates that action to halt such erosion may be justified" (Source, same as table 5) Noncritical erosion does not mean insignificant: "Many noncritical eroding shores in all probability would have been classified critical if development had occurred close to the shore." (Source, same as table 5).

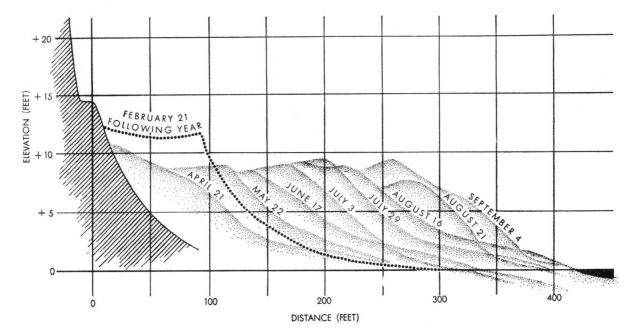

EROSION AND DEPOSITION OPERATE SEASONALLY. The processes of erosion and deposition can work in the same place but at different seasons. This figure shows the growth and erosion of a beach near Carmel, California by a series of dated slopes, based on actual measurements. Vertical dimension is exaggerated ten times. The dotted line shows how the berm was cut back during the following winter. (From "Beaches," by Willard Bascom. Copyright © 1960 by Scientific American, Inc. All rights reserved.)

Table 5. LENGTH OF ERODING SHORELINE BY STATE.

| State or Region | Total Shoreline | Critically eroding Miles | % | Non critically eroding Miles | % | Signif- icantly eroding[1] % | Not eroding Miles | % |
|---|---|---|---|---|---|---|---|---|
| Maine | 2,500 | 20 | | 2,475 | 99 | 99 | 5 | |
| New Hampshire | 40 | 2 | 5 | 36 | 90 | 95 | 2 | 5 |
| Massachusetts | 1,200 | 135 | 11 | 1,030 | 86 | 97 | 35 | 3 |
| Rhode Island | 340 | 5 | 7 | 310 | 91 | 98 | 5 | 1 |
| Connecticut | 270 | 25 | 9 | 240 | 89 | 98 | 5 | 2 |
| New York | 638 | 299 | 47 | 399 | 53 | 100 | 0 | 0 |
| New Jersey | 469 | 122 | 26 | 110 | 23 | 49 | 237 | 51 |
| Delaware | 226 | 28 | 12 | 31 | 14 | 26 | 167 | 74 |
| Maryland | 1,939 | 180 | 9 | 1,500 | 77 | 86 | 259 | 13 |
| Virginia | 993 | 258 | 26 | 300 | 30 | 56 | 435 | 44 |
| North Carolina | 3,661 | 539 | 15 | 723 | 20 | 35 | 2,399 | 66 |
| South Carolina | 3,063 | 57 | 2 | 191 | 6 | 8 | 2,815 | 92 |
| Georgia | 204 | 7 | 4 | 37 | 18 | 22 | 160 | 78 |
| Florida | 6,266 | 292 | 5 | 690 | 11 | 16 | 5,284 | 84 |
| Alabama | 352 | 33 | 9 | 111 | 32 | 41 | 206 | 59 |
| Mississippi | 247 | 37 | 15 | 69 | 28 | 43 | 142 | 57 |
| Louisiana | 1,943 | 29 | 2 | 1,554 | 80 | 82 | 360 | 19 |
| Texas | 2,498 | 93 | 4 | 259 | 10 | 14 | 2,146 | 86 |
| California | 1,827 | 80 | 4 | 1,487 | 81 | 85 | 260 | 14 |
| Oregon | 500 | 64 | 13 | 102 | 20 | 33 | 335 | 67 |
| Washington | 2,337 | 7 | * | 91 | 4 | 4 | 2,239 | 96 |
| TOTAL | 31,513 | 2,332 | 7 | 11,685 | 37 | 45 | 17,496 | 55 |
| | | | | | | | | |
| Maine to Virginia | 8,615 | 1,094 | 13 | 6,371 | 74 | 87 | 1,150 | 13 |
| North Carolina to Georgia | 6,928 | 603 | 9 | 951 | 14 | 22 | 5,374 | 78 |
| Florida to Texas | 11,306 | 484 | 4 | 2,683 | 24 | 28 | 8,138 | 72 |
| Pacific | 4,664 | 151 | 3 | 1,680 | 36 | 39 | 2,834 | 61 |

*Less than 1%
[1]Significantly eroding = critically eroding and non critically eroding.
  Source:  U.S. Army Corps of Engineers.  1971.  The National Shoreline Study.

# 6. EROSION CONTROL

To September 30, 1978, $109 million have been spent for Federal/local cooperative beach protection projects authorized by The Congress and managed by the U.S. Army Corps of Engineers. The purpose of most projects has been to forestall beach erosion, a process driven by powerful natural forces that often frustrates the most advanced engineering technology. While groins, bulkheads, and seawalls are imperfect solutions because they go against nature, people who have already built too close to the sea often have no better solution. Table 6 presents the total reported costs by the Corps for beach protection but does not include elaborate inlet navigation projects with their jetties and seawalls, which could otherwise be classified as beach erosion control measures.

Table 6.  EXPENDITURES ON BEACH EROSION CONTROL PROJECTS.

| State | No. of Projects | Construction Costs Total Federal | Local Contribution[1] | Percent Local |
|---|---|---|---|---|
| Maine | 0 | --- | --- | --- |
| New Hampshire | 2 | 821,583 | 325,999 | 28 |
| Massachusetts | 8 | 2,360,178 | 1,450,245 | 38 |
| Rhode Island | 3 | 1,066,261 | 345,146 | 24 |
| Connecticut | 18 | 2,312,104 | 1,047,195 | 31 |
| New York | 2 | 19,772,153 | 13,872,883 | 41 |
| New Jersey | 5 | 2,945,601 | 1,146,325 | 28 |
| Delaware | 2 | 329,365 | 0 | 0 |
| Maryland | 1 | 97,750 | 80,648 | 45 |
| Virginia | 3 | 2,256,366 | 385,845 | 15 |
| North Carolina | 1 | 620,000 | 0 | 0 |
| South Carolina | 1 | 1,535,352 | 637,336 | 29 |
| Georgia | 1 | 2,137,738 | 2,024,856 | 49 |
| Florida | 13 | 17,998,725 | 9,765,976 | 35 |
| Alabama | 0 | --- | --- | --- |
| Mississippi | 1 | 1,133,000 | 0 | 0 |
| Louisiana | 0 | --- | --- | --- |
| Texas | 1 | 1,543,344 | 1,543,344 | 50 |
| California | 12 | 9,244,867 | 4,370,646 | 32 |
| Oregon | 0 | --- | --- | --- |
| Washington | 1 | 5,868,378 | 225,069 | 4 |
| TOTAL | | 72,042,165 | 37,221,513 | 34 |

TOTAL FEDERAL
AND LOCAL                          109,263,678

---

[1] Operation and maintenance costs assumed by local authorities and not listed here.
Source:  Adapted from U.S. Army Corps of Engineers, Chief of Engineers. FY 1978 Annual Report, Volume II, Field Reports.

# 7. BARRIER ISLANDS

Barrier islands pose special beach problems. These are the long low sandy islands located off mainland coasts. They are a subclassification of barrier structures which includes spits and peninsulas having many of the same planning problems as the barrier islands we list here. A few notable examples of barrier structures are: Guano Spit, 32 miles long in St. Johns County, Florida; Cape San Blas Spit, 20.4 miles long in Gulf County, Florida; Gulf Shores (Mobile Point Spit), 29.4 miles long in Baldwin County, Alabama; and Matagorda Peninsula, 51.4 miles long in Matagorda County, Texas. There are many others as well. Barrier islands range from wild and isolated to heavily urbanized. Galveston, Atlantic City, Miami Beach, and Hatteras are examples of cities located on barrier islands. Active barrier islands are fronted by ocean beaches, and often backed by extensive marshes or mangrove swamps. These islands take the brunt of the ocean's force, and so provide a buffer between the mainland and the seas. They change constantly in shape and size as well as in number, as new inlets open, or old inlets close. This dynamic feature drew the Department of the Interior to conclude that permanent human habitation of many barrier islands is hazardous.[1] This same report lists almost 300 barrier islands, from which we selected for Table 7 true barrier islands generally over 500 acres in highland area, based on an earlier report (See Table 7 for source). Some no longer appear as islands, having recently become part of the mainland. A few (the sea islands of Georgia) are not strictly barrier islands, because they are Pleistocene rather than Holocene formations; i.e., they are composed of older sediments than the true barrier islands.

[1] U.S. Department of the Interior, Heritage Conservation and Recreation Service. 1980. Alternative Policies for Protecting Barrier Islands Along the Atlantic and Gulf Coasts of the United States, and Draft Environmental Impact Statement. Washington, D.C. 20243.

Table 7.  CHARACTERISTICS OF MAJOR BARRIER ISLANDS (ATLANTIC AND GULF COASTS).

| State/Island Name | Length | Access | County |
|---|---|---|---|
| **Atlantic Coast Barrier Islands** | | | |
| **Massachusetts** | | | |
| Plum Island | 8.4 | Bridge | Essex |
| Monomoy Island | 8.9 | Boat | Barnstable |
| **New York** | | | |
| Westhampton | 15.2 | 3 Bridges | Suffolk |
| Fire Island | 53.4 | Ferries, 2 Bridges | Suffolk |
| Jones Beach Island | 14.5 | 3 Bridges | Suffolk and Nassau |
| Long Beach Island | 9.5 | 3 Bridges | Nassau |
| **New Jersey** | | | |
| Sandy Hook | 12.7 | Bridges, Ferry, Highway | Monmouth |
| Island Beach | 20.9 | 3 Bridges | Ocean |
| Long Beach Island | 20.2 | 1 Bridge | Ocean |
| Pullen Island | 4.3 | Boat | Atlantic |
| Brigantine | 8.2 | 1 Bridge | Atlantic |
| Absecon | 8.3 | 6 Bridges | Atlantic |
| Peck Beach | 8.4 | 4 Bridges | Cape May |
| Ludlam Beach | 3.5 | 3 Bridges | Cape May |
| Seven Mile Beach | 7.7 | 4 Bridges | Cape May |
| Wildwood | 6.6 | 3 Bridges | Cape May |
| **Delaware** | | | |
| Fenwick Island (Delaware portion) | 6.1 | Highway | Sussex |
| **Maryland** | | | |
| Fenwick Island (Maryland portion) | 8.8 | 2 Bridges, Highway | Worcester |
| Assateague Island (Maryland portion) | 21.7 | 1 Bridge | Worcester |
| **Virginia** | | | |
| Assateague Island (Virginia portion) | 13.3 | 1 Bridge | Accomack |
| Wallops Island | 6.5 | Causeway | Accomack |
| Metomkin Island | 6.6 | Boat | Accomack |
| Cedar Island | 6.6 | Boat | Accomack |

Table 7. CHARACTERISTICS OF MAJOR BARRIER ISLANDS (ATLANTIC AND GULF COASTS). (cont.)

| State/Island Name | Length | Access | County |
|---|---|---|---|
| Virginia (cont.) | | | |
| Parramore Island | 8.4 | Boat | Accomack |
| Hog Island | 6.9 | Boat | Northampton |
| Cobb Island | 5.9 | Boat | Northampton |
| Smith Island | 8.1 | Boat | Northampton |
| Fishermen's Island | 4.8 | Bridge (exit closed) | Northampton |
| | | | |
| North Carolina | | | |
| Bodie Island | 32.8 | 2 Bridges | Dare |
| Hatteras Island | 49.7 | 2 Bridges, Ferry | Dare |
| Ocracoke Island | 16.6 | 2 Ferries | Hyde |
| Portsmouth Island | 8.7 | Ferry | Carteret |
| Core Banks N. | 11.9 | Boat | Carteret |
| Core Banks S. | 22.5 | Boat | Carteret |
| Shackleford Banks | 9.2 | Boat | Carteret |
| Bogue Banks | 26.3 | 2 Bridges | Carteret |
| Hammock Island | 3.8 | Passenger Ferry | Onslow |
| Onslow Beach | 14.0 | Bridge | Onslow |
| Topsail (Ashe) Island | 21.9 | 2 Bridges | Onslow/Pender |
| Figure Eight Island | 4.4 | Private Bridge | Pender/New Hanover |
| Wrightsville Beach and Shell Island | 4.7 | Bridge | New Hanover |
| Masonboro Island | 8.0 | Boat | New Hanover |
| Carolina Beach Island | 11.1 | Bridge | New Hanover/Brunswick |
| Smith Island and Bald Head Island | 10.5 | Boat | Brunswick |
| Oak Island | 12.7 | Bridge | Brunswick |
| Holden Beach Island | 8.1 | Bridge | Brunswick |
| Hales Beach Island | 5.9 | 2 Bridges | Brunswick |
| Sunset Beach Island | 2.7 | Bridge | Brunswick |
| | | | |
| South Carolina | | | |
| Waites Island | 2.3 | Footbridge | Horry |
| North Island | 8.2 | Unimproved Causeway | Georgetown |
| South Island | 4.9 | Unimproved Causeway, Ferry | Georgetown |
| Murphy Island | 4.4 | Boat | Charleston |
| Cape Island | 5.4 | Boat | Charleston |

Table 7.  CHARACTERISTICS OF MAJOR BARRIER ISLANDS (ATLANTIC AND GULF COASTS)
(cont.).

| State/Island Name | Length | Access | County |
|---|---|---|---|
| **South Carolina (cont.)** | | | |
| Bull Island | 7.1 | Ferries | Charleston |
| Capers Island | 3.1 | Boat | Charleston |
| Isle of Palms | 6.9 | Bridge | Charleston |
| Folly Island | 6.5 | Bridge | Charleston |
| Kiawah Island | 10.1 | Bridge | Charleston |
| Seabrook Island | 1.9 | Bridge | Charleston |
| Edisto Island | 5.8 | Bridge | Charleston |
| Hunting Island | 4.2 | Bridge | Beaufort |
| Fripp Island | 3.9 | Bridge | Beaufort |
| Pritchards/Long Island | 2.6 | Boat | Beaufort |
| St. Phillips Island | 1.2 | Boat | Beaufort |
| Hilton Head Island | 13.8 | Bridge, Airport | Beaufort |
| Dafuskie Island | 3.7 | Boat | Beaufort |
| **Georgia** | | | |
| Savannah Beach | 3.2 | Bridge | Chatham |
| Tybee Island | 5.6 | Boat | Chatham |
| Wassaw Island | 6.1 | Boat | Chatham |
| Ossabaw Island | 10.2 | Boat | Chatham |
| St. Catherines Island | 10.7 | Boat | Bryan |
| Blackbeard Island | 8.0 | Boat | McIntosh |
| Sapelo Island | 5.8 | Ferry | McIntosh |
| Little St. Simons Island | 7.8 | Boat | McIntosh/Glynn |
| St. Simons Island | 4.3 | Causeway | Glynn |
| Jekyll Island | 8.4 | Causeway, Bridge | Glynn |
| Little Cumberland Island | 2.8 | Boat | Glynn |
| Cumberland Island | 16.6 | Ferry | Glynn |
| **Florida** | | | |
| Amelia Island | 13.0 | 2 Bridges | Nassau |
| Little Talbot Island | 7.0 | 2 Bridges | Duval |
| Anastasia Island | 14.5 | 3 Bridges | St. Johns |
| Canaveral | 53.8 | Bridge, Causeway, Railroad | Volusia/Brevard |
| Cocoa Beach Island | 39.2 | 8 Bridges, Causeways | Brevard |
| Vero Beach Island | 28.5 | 5 Bridges, Causeways | Indian R./St. Lucie |

Table 7.  CHARACTERISTICS OF MAJOR BARRIER ISLANDS (ATLANTIC AND GULF COASTS)
(cont.).

| State/Island Name | Length | Access | County |
|---|---|---|---|
| **Florida (cont.)** | | | |
| Hutchison Island | 22.4 | 4 Bridges, Causeways | St. Lucie/Martin |
| Jupiter Island | 16.1 | 2 Bridges | Martin/Palm Beach |
| Lake Worth | 12.1 | 2 Bridges | Palm Beach |
| Palm Beach | 15.6 | 6 Bridges | Palm Beach |
| Boca Raton | 14.5 | 3 Bridges | Palm Beach |
| Hillsboro Beach | 5.5 | 3 Bridges | Palm Beach/Broward |
| Ft. Lauderdale | 11.3 | 3 Bridges | Broward |
| Hollywood Beach | 13.2 | Bridges | Broward |
| Miami Beach | 9.4 | 6 Bridges | Dade |
| Virginia Key | 1.8 | Bridge | Dade |
| Key Biscayne | 4.8 | Bridge | Dade |

Number of Atlantic Coast Barrier Islands = 93

**Gulf of Mexico Barrier Islands**
**Florida**

| | | | |
|---|---|---|---|
| Cape Romano/Kice Island | 4.8 | Boat | Collier |
| Marco Island | 4.6 | 2 Bridges | Collier |
| Keewaydin Group | 9.3 | Boat | Collier |
| Bonita Beach | 5.6 | Bridge | Collier/Lee |
| Lover's Key Group | 2.7 | 2 Bridges | Lee |
| Estero Island | 7.1 | 2 Bridges | Lee |
| Sanibel Island | 11.2 | Causeway, Bridge | Lee |
| Captiva Island | 6.2 | Bridge | Lee |
| North Captiva Island | 4.2 | Boat | Lee |
| Cayo Costa | 8.0 | Boat | Lee |
| Gasparilla Island | 6.9 | 2 Bridges, Railroad | Lee/Charlotte |
| Bocilla Island | 6.2 | Boat | Charlotte |
| Manasota Key | 13.3 | 3 Bridges | Charlotte/Sarasota |
| Casey Key | 7.1 | 2 Bridges | Sarasota |
| Siesta Key | 7.3 | 2 Bridges | Sarasota |
| Lido Key | 2.3 | 2 Bridges | Sarasota |
| Longboat | 10.4 | 2 Bridges | Sarasota/Manatee |
| Anna Maria Key | 7.6 | 3 Bridges | Manatee |
| Mullet Key | 2.6 | Bridge | Pinellas |
| Long Key | 4.1 | 3 Bridges | Pinellas |
| Treasure Island | 3.5 | 3 Bridges | Pinellas |

Table 7. CHARACTERISTICS OF MAJOR BARRIER ISLANDS (ATLANTIC AND GULF COASTS) (cont.).

| State/Island Name | Length | Access | County |
|---|---|---|---|
| **Florida (cont.)** | | | |
| Sand Key | 14.1 | 4 Bridges | Pinellas |
| Clearwater Beach Island | 3.3 | 3 Bridges | Pinellas |
| Caladesi Island | 2.4 | Boat | Pinellas |
| Anclote Keys | 3.4 | Boat | Pinellas/Pasco |
| Dog Island | 8.0 | Ferry | Franklin |
| St. George Island | 18.7 | Bridge | Franklin |
| Little St. George Island | 10.1 | Boat | Franklin |
| St. Vincent Island | 8.7 | Boat | Franklin |
| Hurricane/Shell Island | 5.9 | Boat | Bay |
| Santa Rosa Island | 47.9 | 4 Bridges | Okaloosa/Escambia |
| Perdido Key (Florida portion) | 13.2 | 2 Bridges | Escambia |
| **Alabama** | | | |
| Perdido Key (Alabama portion) | 1.6 | 2 Bridges | Baldwin |
| Dauphin Island | 13.8 | Bridge | Mobile |
| Little Dauphin Island | 3.5 | Bridge | Mobile |
| **Mississippi** | | | |
| Petit Bois (Pettibone) Island | 7.0 | Boat | Jackson |
| Horn Island | 14.1 | Boat | Jackson |
| Ship Island[1] | 5.7 | Tourboat | Harrison |
| Cat Island | 3.9 | Boat | Harrison |
| **Louisiana** | | | |
| Chandeleur and Breton Islands | 27.8 | Boat | St. Bernard/Plaquemines |
| Grand Isle | 7.2 | Bridge | Jefferson |
| Timbalier Island | 8.3 | Boat | Lafourche/Terrebone |
| Isles Dernieres[2] | 16.2 | Boat | Vermillion/Cameron/Terrebone |

Table 7.  CHARACTERISTICS OF MAJOR BARRIER ISLANDS (ATLANTIC AND GULF COASTS) (cont.)

| State/Island Name | Length | Access | County |
|---|---|---|---|
| Texas | | | |
| Galveston Island | 28.6 | Bridges | Galveston |
| Matagorda Island | 36.2 | Boat, Airfield | Calhoun |
| St. Joseph Island | 19.3 | Boat, Airfield | Aransas/Nueces |
| Mustang Island | 18.0 | Ferry, Bridges | Nueces |
| Padre Island North | 75.1 | Causeway | Nueces/Kleberg/Kenedy |
| Padre Island South | 39.9 | Causeway | Willacy/Cameron |

Number of Gulf Coast Barrier Islands = 55

---

[1] Two islands
[2] Eight islands
Source:  Adopted from John R. Clark, et. al., July 1977.  Review of Major Barrier Islands of the United States.  New York:  The Barrier Islands Workshop;  Robert Peoples, U.S. Fish and Wildlife Service, Washington, D.C.  Pers. comm.

# 8. BARRIER ISLANDS

Over 1500 miles of major barrier islands front the Atlantic and Gulf Coasts. These islands maintain quiet sounds, estuaries or lagoons between themselves and the mainland for fisheries, nurseries for fishes, marshes, and recreation on calmer waters. This table compares the general shoreline to the length of barrier islands fronting each state. Maryland has the highest percentage of its shoreline fronted with barrier islands, because the general shoreline measures only Maryland's ocean coast. North Carolina is second.

Table 8. LENGTH OF BARRIER ISLAND BY STATE.

| State | No. of Islands[1] | Total Length (mi.) | % of General Shoreline[2] |
|---|---|---|---|
| Massachusetts | 2 | 18 | 9 |
| New York | 4 | 93 | 73 |
| New Jersey | 10 | 100 | 77 |
| Delaware | 1 | 6 | 21 |
| Maryland | 2 | 31 | 98 |
| Virginia | 9 | 67 | 60 |
| North Carolina | 20 | 285 | 95 |
| South Carolina | 18 | 96 | 51 |
| Georgia | 12 | 89 | 89 |
| Florida | 49 | 560 | 41 |
| Florida Atlantic | 17 | 283 | 49 |
| Florida Gulf | 32 | 247 | 32 |
| Alabama | 3 | 19 | 86 |

| State or Region | No. of Islands | Total Length (mi.) | % of General Shoreline |
|---|---|---|---|
| Louisiana | 11 | 59 | 15 |
| Texas | 6 | 217 | 59 |
| TOTAL | 147 | 1,610 | 47 |
| Massachusetts to Atlantic Florida | 95 | 1,063 | 50 |
| Massachusetts to Virginia | 28 | 315 | 50 |
| North Carolina to Atlantic Florida | 67 | 753 | 65 |
| Florida Gulf to Texas | 52 | 542 | 35 |

[1] not additive, because some islands are in two states.
[2] U.S. Department of Commerce, NOAA. 1975. The Coastline of the United States; U.S. Army Corps of Engineers. 1971. The National Shoreline Study.

Source: Adopted from John R. Clark, et. al., July 1977. Review of Major Barrier Islands of the United States. New York: The Barrier Islands Workshop; Robert Peoples, U.S. Fish Wildlife Service, Washington, D.C. Pers. comm.

# 9. BARRIER ISLAND DEVELOPMENT

Barrier island change constantly in size and shape. The Department of the Interior has concluded that most are poor places for permanent human habitation.[1] Nevertheless, over one-third of the length of major barrier islands is developed. Development reaches its peak in New Jersey, and is at a minimum in Mississippi. Over one-third of the length of major barrier islands is preserved. Land which is preserved is defined as being owned by an individual or organization which has the intent and the ability to keep its property in an undeveloped state for the forseeable future. The highest proportion of preserved barrier island is on the North Atlantic coast (58%). Over one-quarter of barrier island length is currently uncommitted to either development or preservation, although some of this length is on the verge of development, because it has the facilities, such as roads, power, and sewage which will allow development. Florida has the greatest expanse in this last category.

This information is presented, as is the other information on barrier islands, as length, because we find that the estimates of island area often vary widely between sources, while sources usually agree on length.

[1] See Text to Table 7.

Table 9. DEVELOPMENT STATUS OF MAJOR BARRIER ISLANDS.

| State or Region | Developed Miles | % | Preserved Miles | % | Undeveloped and Unpreserved Miles | % | Undeveloped and unpreserved but with infrastructure for development extant Miles | % |
|---|---|---|---|---|---|---|---|---|
| Massachusetts | 1.8 | 10 | 15.5 | 90 | 0 | 0 | 0 | 0 |
| New York | 38.2 | 41 | 54.5 | 59 | 0 | 0 | 0 | 0 |
| New Jersey | 70.0 | 70 | 24.9 | 24 | 3.8 | 4 | 2.1 | 2 |
| Delaware | 3.0 | 49 | 2.3 | 38 | 0.8 | 13 | 0 | 0 |
| Maryland | 8.8 | 29 | 21.7 | 71 | 0 | 0 | 0 | 0 |
| Virginia | 3.0 | 4 | 64.4 | 96 | 0 | 0 | 0 | 0 |
| North Carolina | 94.7 | 33 | 119.8 | 42 | 47.1 | 17 | 23.8 | 8 |
| South Carolina | 33.2 | 35 | 34.5 | 36 | 21.4 | 22 | 6.9 | 7 |
| Georgia | 15.3 | 18 | 41.4 | 49 | 28.2 | 33 | 0 | 0 |
| Florida | 247.7 | 44 | 89.7 | 16 | 142.9 | 26 | 75.8 | 14 |
| Florida Atlantic | 135.9 | 48 | 28.3 | 10 | 64.2 | 23 | 54.3 | 19 |
| Florida Gulf | 103.8 | 43 | 45.4 | 19 | 72.7 | 30 | 21.5 | 9 |
| Alabama | 6.1 | 32 | 0.5 | 3 | 11.6 | 61 | 0.7 | 4 |
| Mississippi | 0 | 0 | 26.8 | 87 | 3.9 | 13 | 0 | 0 |
| Louisiana | 6.3 | 11 | 28.0 | 47 | 25.2 | 42 | 0 | 0 |
| Texas | 29.0 | 13 | 116.4 | 54 | 55.1 | 25 | 16.6 | 8 |
| TOTAL | 549.1 | 34 | 624.4 | 38 | 334.0 | 20 | 123.8 | 8 |
| | | | | | | | | |
| Atlantic | 403.9 | 38 | 407.3 | 38 | 165.5 | 16 | 87.1 | 8 |
| North Atlantic | 124.8 | 40 | 183.3 | 58 | 4.6 | 1 | 2.1 | * |
| South Atlantic | 279.1 | 37 | 224.0 | 30 | 160.9 | 21 | 85.0 | 11 |
| Gulf | 145.2 | 25 | 217.1 | 38 | 168.5 | 30 | 38.8 | 7 |

* Less than 1%
Source: Adopted from John R. Clark. July 1977. Review of Major Barrier Islands of the United States. New York: The Barrier Islands Workshop; Robert Peoples, U.S. Fish and Wildlife Service, Washington, D.C. pers. comm.

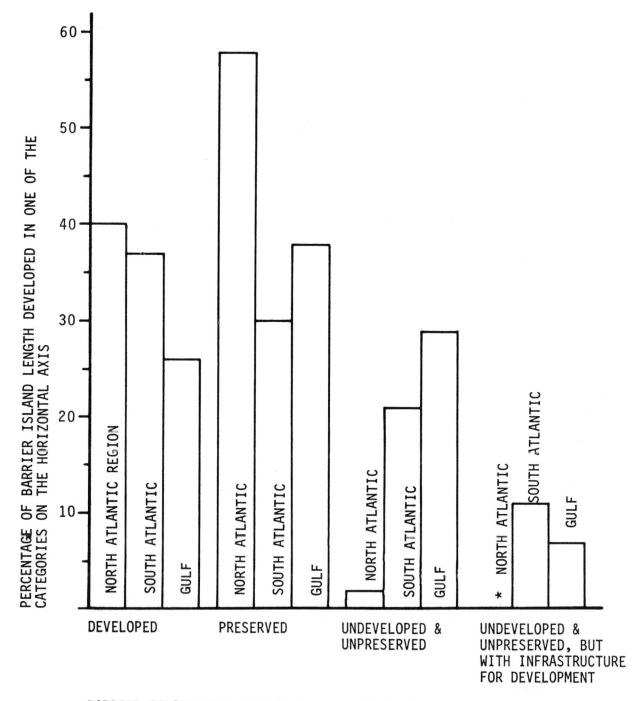

PERCENTAGE OF BARRIER ISLAND LENGTH DEVELOPED IN ONE OF THE CATEGORIES ON THE HORIZONTAL AXIS

60

50

40

30

20

10

NORTH ATLANTIC REGION
SOUTH ATLANTIC
GULF

NORTH ATLANTIC
SOUTH ATLANTIC
GULF

NORTH ATLANTIC
SOUTH ATLANTIC
GULF

* NORTH ATLANTIC
SOUTH ATLANTIC
GULF

DEVELOPED

PRESERVED

UNDEVELOPED & UNPRESERVED

UNDEVELOPED & UNPRESERVED, BUT WITH INFRASTRUCTURE FOR DEVELOPMENT

BARRIER ISLAND DEVELOPMENT by type of development and region. (by Ruth Ann Hill). * Less than 1%

# II  PHYSICAL CHARACTERISTICS

Physical characteristics set a broad framework within which man, other animals, and plants must adapt and live.  The flow of rivers to the sea dilutes in-rushing salt water, and the combination of the two forms estuaries (see Section VI).  The salinity regime in an estuary changes in response to changes in river discharge.  As river discharge varies, the salinity that a sedentary animal will experience also varies.

Sea level changes daily due to solar and lunar tides.  Animals that live within the zone continually covered and uncovered by ebbing and flooding tides--the intertidal zone--are adapted to living now under water, and then under the air for long periods of time.  Fifteen thousand years ago, sea level was 400 feet lower than it is today.

The range of temperatures at some places along the coast is large --over 50 degrees F at some places.  People and animals who use the sea year round must make provisions for this wide range of temperatures.

# 10. RIVER DISCHARGES

Water which evaporates from the oceans and lakes forms the clouds which release rain or snow over land masses. Precipitation runs off the land and finds its way to rivers which flow to the coast. This water cycle has many implications. First, the positioning of <u>salinity</u> gradients in <u>estuaries</u> is controlled in part by river flow. Second, terrestial runoff carries pollutants -- ranging from sediments to fertilizer to pesticides, and other compounds -- into estuaries and the ocean. Third, many organisms have intricate adaptations to reproduction in the expected estuarine flow regimes. Thus, the flow of rivers to the sea is an important physical characteristic.

The information presented in Table 10 refers to the average flow of rivers discharging to coastal waters where those coastal waters are adjacent to the coterminous United States. Thus the St. Lawrence River, for example, which drains the United States is not listed. The flow of each river is highly variable. For example, the mean discharge of the Susquehanna River is about 40,000 cubic feet per second (cfs), but during Hurricane Agnes in June, 1972, its flow exceeded 1,000,000 cfs.

The three rivers with the largest average discharge to the sea in the coterminous United States are (1) The Mississippi at 650,000 cfs (37% of the U.S. total), (2) the Columbia river at 281,200 cfs (16% of the U.S. total), and (3) the Mobile River at 63,160 cfs (4% of the U.S. total).

Table 10. RIVER AND BASIN DISCHARGE TO THE SEAS.

| Basin or River | Area Discharge (cfs)[1] | Area Discharge as a % of U.S. Discharge to Atlantic Ocean | River Discharge (cfs)[1] | River Discharge as a % of Basin Total |
|---|---|---|---|---|
| Passamaquoddy Bay to Penobscot Bay | 23,500 | 6.5 | | |
| Penobscot River | | | 16,750 | 71.3 |
| St. George River to Cape Cod Bay | 41,020 | 11.4 | | |
| Kennebec River | | | 11,210 | 27.3 |
| Androscoggin River | | | 7,229 | 17.6 |
| Saco River | | | 4,040 | 9.8 |
| Merrimack River | | | 9,183 | 22.4 |
| Cape Cod to New York-Connecticut State Line | 34,810 | 9.7 | | |
| Connecticut River | | | 21,400 | 61.5 |
| Housatonic River | | | 3,799 | 10.9 |
| New York-Connecticut State Line to Cape May | 32,770 | 9.1 | | |

Table 10. RIVER AND BASIN DISCHARGE TO THE SEAS (cont.)

| Basin or River | Area Discharge (cfs) | Area Discharge as a % of U.S. Discharge to Atlantic Ocean | River Discharge (cfs) | River Discharge as a % of Basin Total |
|---|---|---|---|---|
| Hudson River and smaller streams | | | 22,700 | 69.3 |
| Cape May to Cape Henry | 101,200 | 28.2 | | |
| Delaware River | | | 19,900 | 19.7 |
| Susquehanna River | | | 40,290 | 39.8 |
| Potomac River | | | 13,700 | 13.5 |
| James River | | | 10,030 | 9.9 |
| Cape Henry to Neuse River | 27,500 | 7.7 | | |
| Chowan River | | | 4,626 | 16.8 |
| Roanoke River | | | 8,620 | 31.3 |
| Pamlico River | | | 4,693 | 17.1 |
| Neuse River | | | 5,703 | 20.7 |
| Cove Sound to Black River | 28,440 | 7.9 | | |
| Cape Fear River | | | 9,475 | 33.3 |
| Pee Dee River | | | 15,270 | 53.7 |
| Santee River to Sapelo Island | 35,290 | 9.8 | | |
| Savannah River | | | 10,280 | 29.1 |
| Ogeechee River | | | 3,513 | 10.0 |
| Altamaha River to Cape Kennedy | 25,860 | 7.2 | | |
| Altamaha River | | | 12,140 | 46.9 |
| St. Johns River | | | 8,868 | 34.3 |
| Cape Kennedy to Cape Sable | 9,000 | 2.5 | | |
| Atlantic Ocean Total | 359,400 | | | |

| Basin or River | Area Discharge (cfs) | Area Discharge as a % of U.S. Discharge to Gulf of Mexico | River Discharge (cfs) | River Discharge as a % of Basin Total |
|---|---|---|---|---|
| Cape Sable to Alligator Creek | 2,500 | 0.3 | | |
| Peace River to New River | 27,200 | 3.1 | | |
| Suwanee River | | | 680 | 39.3 |
| Apalachicola River | 26,700 | 3.0 | | |
| Wetappo Creek to Perdido River | 25,100 | 2.8 | | |
| Choctawhatchee River | | | 7,360 | 29.3 |

25

Table 10.  RIVER AND BASIN DISCHARGE TO THE SEAS (cont.)

| Basin or River | Area Discharge (cfs) | Area Discharge as a % of U.S. Discharge to Gulf of Mexico | River Discharge (cfs) | River Discharge as a % of Basin Total |
|---|---|---|---|---|
| Escambia River | | | 6,880 | 27.4 |
| Mobile Bay | 64,200 | 7.2 | | |
| Mobile Bay | | | 63,160 | 98.4 |
| Pascagoula River to Pearl River | 31,200 | 3.5 | | |
| Pascagoula River | | | 15,200 | 48.7 |
| Pearl River | | | 12.900 | 41.3 |
| Mississippi River | 650,000 | 73.3 | | |
| Vermillion, Mermentau and Calcasie Rivers | 10,800 | 1.2 | | |
| Sabine River to Rio Grande | 49,700 | 5.6 | | |
| Sabine River | | | 9,050 | 18.2 |
| Neches River | | | 8,240 | 16.6 |
| Trinity River | | | 7,490 | 15.1 |
| Brazos River | | | 6,220 | 12.5 |
| Colorado River | | | 3,000 | 6.0 |
| Guadalupe and San Antonio Rivers | | | 2,350 | 4.7 |
| Nueces River | | | 820 | 1.6 |
| Rio Grande | | | 660 | 1.3 |
| Gulf of Mexico Total | 887,400 | | | |

| Basin or River | Area Discharge (cfs) | Area Discharge as a % of U.S. Discharge to Pacific Ocean | River Discharge (cfs) | River Discharge as a % of Basin Total |
|---|---|---|---|---|
| Colorado River | 200 | 0.04 | | |
| Tia Juana River to Ventura River | 500 | 0.1 | | |
| San Jose Creek to Pesadero Creek | 2,400 | 0.5 | | |
| San Francisco Bay | 30,400 | 6.1 | | |
| Lagunitas Creek to Smith River | 42,100 | 8.4 | | |
| Eel River | | | 9,120 | 21.7 |
| Klamath River | | | 17,100 | 40.6 |
| Smith River | | | 4,360 | 10.4 |

26

Table 10.  RIVER AND BASIN DISCHARGE TO THE SEAS (cont.)

| Basin or River | Area Discharge (cfs) | Area Discharge as a % of U.S. Discharge to Pacific Ocean | River Discharge (cfs) | River Discharge as a % of Basin Total |
|---|---|---|---|---|
| Oregon Coastal Area | 53,300 | 10.7 | | |
| Rogue River | | | 11,000 | 20.6 |
| Umpqua River | | | 10,700 | 20.1 |
| Columbia River | 281,200 | 56.4 | | |
| Naselle River to Nooksack River | 89,100 | 17.8 | | |
| Chehalis River | | | 7,730 | 8.7 |
| Queets River | | | 4,120 | 4.6 |
| Snohomish River | | | 8,800 | 9.9 |
| Skagit River | | | 16,350 | 18.4 |
| Nooksack River | | | 3,720 | 4.2 |
| | | | | |
| Pacific Ocean Total | 499,200 | | | |
| Coterminous United States Total | 1,746,000 | | | |

---

[1] cfs is cubic feet per second which equals 448.8 gallons per minute

Source:  Alfonso Wilson and Kathleen T. Iseri.  1969.  River Discharge to the Sea from the Shores of the Conterminous United States, Alaska, and Puerto Rico.  U.S. Department of the Interior, U.S. Geological Survey, Hydrologic Investigations Atlas HA-282.

# 11. SEA LEVEL CHANGES

The sea has been slowly and relentlessly rising from polar ice melt. Changes in relative sealevel along U.S. coasts are due not only to the change in height of sealevel, but also to the changes in the level of the land. From both causes, relative sealevel is rising -- at over 2 feet per century at Galveston, Texas; but, in isolated cases, decreasing at over 4 feet per century in Juneau, Alaska.

Many of our nation's coasts have shallow slopes that rise gradually. Relatively small changes in sealevel in these areas can drastically alter the extent of exposed or submerged lands. For example, on a coast with a 1 degree slope, a 20-inch vertical drop in sealevel would move the shoreline over 30 yards seaward.

Table 11. CHANGES IN SEA LEVEL OBSERVED AT SELECTED COASTAL POINTS.

| | cm/ decade | inches/ century | | cm/ decade | inches/ century |
|---|---|---|---|---|---|
| Northeast Coast | | | Southeast Coast | | |
| Portland, ME | 2.2 | 8.66 | Charleston, SC | 3.8 | 14.96 |
| Eastport, ME | 3.3 | 12.99 | Savannah, GA | 3.1 | 12.20 |
| Boston, MA | 2.8 | 11.02 | Miami Beach, FL | 2.6 | 10.24 |
| Woods Hole, MA | 3.3 | 12.99 | Gulf Coast | | |
| Newport, RI | 3.0 | 11.81 | Key West, FL | 2.3 | 9.06 |
| New London, CT | 2.6 | 10.24 | Pensacola, FL | 2.7 | 10.63 |
| Montauk, NY | 2.6 | 10.24 | Galveston, TX | 6.3 | 24.80 |
| New York, NY | 2.9 | 11.42 | Pacific Coast | | |
| Sandy Hook, NJ | 4.9 | 19.29 | La Jolla, CA | 1.7 | 6.69 |
| Atlantic City, NJ | 4.1 | 16.14 | Los Angelos, CA | 0.5 | 1.97 |
| Lewes, DE | 3.7 | 14.57 | San Francisco, CA | 1.3 | 5.12 |
| Philadelphia, PA | 2.8 | 11.02 | Astoria, OR | -0.1 | -0.39 |
| Annapolis, MD | 4.2 | 16.54 | Seattle, WA | 1.9 | 7.48 |
| Solomons, MD | 4.0 | 15.75 | Friday Harbor, WA | 1.0 | 3.94 |
| Norfolk, VA | 4.7 | 18.50 | Juneau, AK | -13.4 | -52.76 |
| | | | Ketchikan, AK | -0.2 | -0.79 |

Source: Modified from Steacy D. Hicks, March 20, 1978. An average geopotential Sea Level Series for the United States. J. Geophysical Research, Vol. 83, 1377-1379.

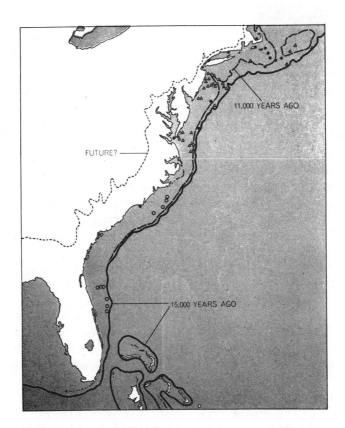

ATLANTIC COAST SHORELINE HAS VARIED GREATLY in the past and will undoubtedly continue to in the future.  This illustration compares the shoreline of 15,000 and 11,000 years ago with the probable shoreline if all the ice at the poles were to melt.  Confirmation that the continental shelf was once laid bare is found in discoveries of elephant teeth (triangles), freshwater peat (dots) and the shallow-water formations called oolites (circles).

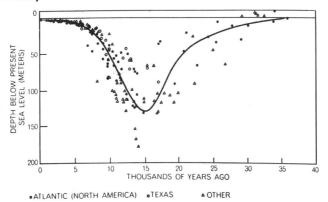

• ATLANTIC (NORTH AMERICA)   • TEXAS   ▲ OTHER

WORLDWIDE CHANGES IN SEA LEVEL can be inferred from the radiocarbon ages of shallow-water marine organisms and the depth at which they were recovered.  Samples are from the Atlantic shelf of North America, the Texas shelf and other parts of the world.  The depth inconsistency of the Texas samples implies that the shelf there has been uplifted.
(Both figures from "The Continental Shelves," by K. O. Emery. Copyright © 1969 by Scientific American, Inc. All rights reserved.)

# 12. TIDE RANGES

The ebb and flood of the tide is one of the fascinating characteristics of the coast. Tides flood and drain many coastal wetlands and other inter-tidal areas, alternately subjecting the plants and animals to ocean waters, and the air. They produce currents (which often exceed three knots) in coastal waters which can be a detriment or an advantage to the mariner.

Tides are produced by the pull of the sun and the moon on the earth, and by the centrifugal force which produces a high tide on the side of the planet opposite the sun and the moon. The effect of the sun is about one-half that of the moon (0.46), because of the greater distance from the sun to the earth. In some places, the tide are semidiurnal, that is, there are two high and two low tides per day. In other places, the tides are diurnal, that is, there is only one high and one low tide per day. In either case, the tidal patttern repeats itself every 24 hours and 50 minutes (the length of a lunar cycle). When the sun and the moon are in line, which is the case during new and full moons, they produce high high tides, and low low tides termed "spring tides." When the sun and the moon are perpendicular to one another, they produce lower high tides, and higher low tides termed "neap tides." There are about two weeks between spring tides, and about two weeks between neap tides. Freshwater flow, winds, and extremes of barometric pressure can alter the expected tide pattern.

In this table, "mean range" is the difference between mean high and mean low waters. "Spring range" is the average range of tides which are the result of new and full moons. "Diurnal range" is the difference in height between mean higher high water, and mean lower low water in areas subject to diurnal tides. Of the stations given here, the maximum mean range is 26.1 feet in Anchorage, Alaska, or in the coterminous United States the maximum mean range is 18.2 feet in Eastport, Maine. The Bay of Fundy in Nova Scotia, Canada has the highest mean tide range in the world -- 38.4 feet -- and a spring tide range in excess of 43 feet.

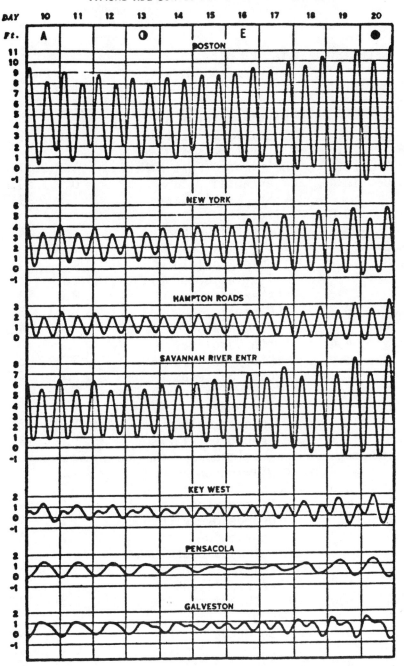

TYPICAL TIDE CURVES FOR UNITED STATES PORTS

Lunar data:
A — Moon in apogee
◑ — last quarter
E — Moon on Equator
● — new Moon

THE PATTERN OF TIDE at various places along the coast. Note that the largest amplitude of tides is near new or full moons. Pensacola tides are diurnal tides -- one high and one low tide per day. The patterns depicted above Pensacola are semi-diurnal tide patterns -- two highs and two lows per day. The pattern at Galveston is a mixed pattern -- sometimes diurnal and sometimes semi-diurnal. (Figure from same source as Table 12.)

31

Table 12. TIDE RANGES FOR SELECTED COASTAL POINTS.

| | Mean (ft) | Spring (ft) |
|---|---|---|
| Maine | | |
| Eastport | 18.2 | 20.7 |
| Bar Harbor | 10.5 | 12.1 |
| Portland | 9.0 | 10.4 |
| New Hampshire | | |
| Portsmouth | 7.8 | 9.0 |
| Massachusetts | | |
| Boston | 9.0 | 10.4 |
| Woods Hole | 1.8 | 2.2 |
| (Oceanographic Institution) | | |
| Cape Cod Lighthouse | 7.6 | 8.8 |
| Rhode Island | | |
| Newport | 3.5 | 4.4 |
| Block Island | 2.9 | 3.6 |
| (Old Harbor) | | |
| Connecticut | | |
| New London | 2.6 | 3.1 |
| (State Pier) | | |
| New Haven | 6.2 | 7.1 |
| (Harbor entrance) | | |
| New York | | |
| Port Chester | 7.2 | 8.5 |
| Brooklyn Bridge | 4.3 | 5.2 |
| Port Jefferson | 6.6 | 7.6 |
| Fire Island | 4.1 | 5.0 |
| Breakwater | | |
| New Jersey | | |
| Sandy Hook | 4.6 | 5.6 |
| Atlantic City | 4.1 | 5.0 |
| (Steel Pier) | | |
| Cape May Harbor | 4.4 | 5.3 |
| Delaware | | |
| Rehoboth Beach | 3.9 | 4.7 |
| Cape Henlopen | 4.1 | 4.9 |
| Maryland | | |
| Ocean City | 3.4 | 4.1 |
| Maryland (cont.) | | |
| Crisfield (Little Annemessex River) | 2.0 | 2.4 |
| Baltimore (Fort McHenry) | 1.1 | 1.3 |
| Annapolis | 0.9 | 1.0 |
| St. Mary's City | 1.5 | 1.7 |
| Virginia | | |
| Assateague Beach (Tom's Cove) | 3.6 | 4.4 |
| Ship Shoal Inlet | 4.0 | 4.8 |
| Tangier Sound Light | 1.6 | 1.9 |
| Alexandria | 2.8 | 3.2 |
| Norfolk | 2.8 | 3.4 |
| Virginia Beach | 3.4 | 4.1 |
| North Carolina | | |
| Kitty Hawk (Ocean) | 3.2 | 3.8 |
| Cape Hatteras | 3.6 | 4.3 |
| Albemarle and Pamlico Sounds | | |
| Oracoke Inlet | 1.9 | 2.3 |
| Beaufort (Pivers Island | 3.0 | 3.6 |
| Wilmington | 4.2 | 4.5 |
| South Carolina | | |
| Myrtle Beach | 5.1 | 6.0 |
| Georgetown Lighthouse | 3.8 | 4.4 |
| Charleston (Customhouse Wharf) | 5.2 | 6.1 |
| Folly Island | 5.2 | 6.1 |
| Parris Island (Beaufort River) | 7.1 | 8.3 |
| Georgia | | |
| Savannah | 7.4 | 8.6 |
| Sapelo Island | 6.8 | 8.0 |
| Jekyll Point | 6.6 | 7.7 |
| Florida (Atlantic Coast and Keys) | | |
| Jacksonville (Dredge Depot) | 2.0 | 2.3 |

Table 12. TIDE RANGES FOR SELECTED COASTAL POINTS (cont.)

| | Mean (ft) | Spring (ft) | | Mean (ft) | Diurnal (ft) |
|---|---|---|---|---|---|
| Florida (cont.) | | | Texas (cont.) | | |
| Cape Canaveral | 3.5 | 4.1 | Pass Cavallo | -- | 1.4 |
| Ft. Lauderdale | 2.3 | 2.8 | Aransas Pass Channel | -- | 1.4 |
| (Bahia Mar Yacht Club) | | | Port Isabel | -- | 1.3 |
| Miami Beach | 2.5 | 3.0 | (Pacific Coast) | | |
| Key West | 1.3 | 1.6 | Washington State | | |
| | | | Seattle | 7.6 | 11.3 |
| | Mean (ft) | Diurnal (ft) | Friday Harbor, | 4.5 | 7.7 |
| (Gulf Coast) | | | San Juan Island | | |
| Everglades City | 2.0 | 2.6 | Bay City, Grays Harbor | 7.1 | 9.2 |
| Naples | 2.1 | 2.8 | Oregon | | |
| Sarasota | -- | 2.1 | Coos Bay | 5.6 | 7.3 |
| Clearwater | 1.8 | 2.6 | Astoria | 6.5 | 8.2 |
| Apalachicola | -- | 1.7 | California | | |
| Pensacola | -- | 1.3 | Cape Mendocino | 4.0 | 5.7 |
| Alabama | | | Alcatraz Island | 4.1 | 5.8 |
| Mobile | -- | 1.5 | Carmel Cove, Carmel Bay | 3.5 | 5.2 |
| Mississippi | | | Santa Barbara | 3.6 | 5.3 |
| Biloxi | -- | 1.8 | Los Angeles | 3.8 | 5.4 |
| Louisiana | | | (Outer Harbor) | | |
| Chandeleur Light | -- | 1.2 | San Clemente | 3.7 | 5.3 |
| Timbalier Island | -- | 1.2 | Point Loma | 3.7 | 5.3 |
| Mermentau River | -- | 2.5 | Alaska | | |
| (entrance) | | | Sitka | 7.7 | 9.9 |
| Texas | | | Juneau | 13.8 | 16.4 |
| Sabine Bank | -- | 2.8 | Port Valdez | 9.7 | 12.0 |
| (Lighthouse) | | | Anchorage | 26.1 | 29.0 |
| Galveston | -- | 1.4 | Hawaii | | |
| (Galveston Channel) | | | Honolulu | 1.2 | 1.9 |

Source: U.S. Department of Commerce, NOAA, NOS, Tide Tables: 1978 High and Low Water Predictions East Coast of North and South America (Including Greenland); Tide Tables: 1978 High and Low Water Predictions West Coast of North and South America (Including the Hawaiian Islands).

# 13. SEA TEMPERATURE

Ocean temperature near the poles, the tropics, and in the depths of the ocean does not fluctuate much on an annual basis. The temperate zone oceans on the other hand vary enormously on an annual basis. A 57-year record of temperatures at Charleston, South Carolina, reveals a 41 degree F difference between mean February and mean August sea temperatures. The same location has a 49 degree F difference between recorded maximum and minimum water temperatures. The east coast and west coast differ a good deal in the variability of temperature. The six stations in California show a 34 degree difference between recorded maximum and minimum temperatures within the entire state. Many single locations on the Atlantic or Gulf coasts display a 40 degree difference between mean temperatures, and a 50 degree difference between extreme temperatures.

Temperature variations are important, because they dictate a very broad range of temperature adaptations that long-lived temperate zone animals must have. These temperature fluctuations are sufficiently regular, that many animals use them for proximate cues in their reproduction and migration cycles as well as in other activities.

Ocean temperatures are determined by the amount of sun that an area receives, as well as the length of time over which it receives sunlight. Ocean currents that may reach an area also influence temperature. The warm Gulf Stream current, and the cool California current markedly effect the temperature along the Atlantic and Pacific coasts.


CENTRIGRADE AND FAHRENHEIT EQUIVALENTS.

| °C | °F | General Formulae: | °F = 9/5  °C + 32 |
|----|----|----|----|
| 0 | 32 | | °C = 5/9 (°F - 32) |
| 5 | 41 | | |
| 10 | 50 | | |
| 15 | 59 | | |
| 20 | 68 | | |
| 25 | 77 | | |
| 30 | 86 | | |
| 35 | 95 | | |
| 40 | 104 | | |

[1] from 1887 to 1893 is not used here
[2] no data collected 1947 to 1953
[3] to 1877

Source:  U.S. Department of Commerce, NOAA, Tidal Datums and
Information Branch, Tides and Water Levels Division.

Table 13.  SEA SURFACE WATER TEMPERATURES FOR SELECTED COASTAL POINTS (°F).[4]

| | FEBRUARY | | | AUGUST | | | year of first record |
|---|---|---|---|---|---|---|---|
| | max. | coldest monthly average | min. | max. | warmest monthly average | min. | |
| Eastport, ME | 40 | 30.7 | 28 | 57 | 54.5 | 46 | 1929 |
| Portsmouth, NH | 40 | 31.6 | 30 | 69 | 64.6 | 50 | 1944 |
| Boston, MA | 52 | 29.8 | 28 | 75 | 70.7 | 50 | 1921 |
| Woods Hole, MA | 39 | 29.5 | 27 | 77 | 73.2 | 66 | 1944 |
| Newport, RI | 42 | 32.5 | 28 | 78 | 72.4 | 64 | 1955 |
| New London, CT | 43 | 33.6 | 31 | 80 | 75.8 | 67 | 1947 |
| Bridgeport, CT | 48 | 33.0 | 30 | 86 | 81.4 | 70 | 1964 |
| Montauk, NY | 41 | 30.3 | 29 | 79 | 72.6 | 62 | 1947 |
| Willets Pt., NY | 46 | 29.5 | 28 | 81 | 75.1 | 64 | 1931 |
| NY (The Battery), NY | 44 | 31.3 | 29 | 79 | 77.2 | 66 | 1926 |
| Sandy Hook, NJ | 45 | 30.7 | 28 | 83 | 78.0 | 68 | 1944[1] |
| Atlantic City, NJ | 44 | 29.8 | 28 | 80 | 76.1 | 57 | 1911 |
| Cape May, NJ | 45 | 34.0 | 28 | 80 | 75.9 | 66 | 1965 |
| Philadelphia, PA | 46 | 32.5 | -- | 86 | 82.8 | -- | 1922[2] |
| Lewes, DE | 47 | 31.5 | 29 | 83 | 77.5 | 67 | 1947 |
| Solomons, MD | 46 | 33.1 | 30 | 87 | 82.8 | 72 | 1937 |
| Baltimore, MD | 45 | 32.4 | 31 | 86 | 82.0 | 71 | 1914 |
| Washington, DC | 52 | 33.8 | 32 | 90 | 85.1 | 73 | 1944 |
| Kiptopeke Beach, VA | 51 | 34.1 | 28 | 85 | 81.0 | 68 | 1951 |
| Myrtle Beach, SC | 60 | 44.1 | 40 | 89 | 85.0 | 73 | 1951 |
| Charleston, SC | 63 | 44.8 | 40 | 89 | 85.8 | 76 | 1921 |
| Ft. Pulaski, GA | 64 | 45.8 | 41 | 89 | 86.2 | 78 | 1939 |
| Fernandina, FL | 70 | 50.9 | 44 | 90 | 86.0 | 75 | 1944 |
| Miami Beach, FL | 79 | 64.0 | 58 | 92 | 88.8 | 82 | 1939 |
| St. Petersburg, FL | 76 | 55.4 | 50 | 90 | 87.4 | 80 | 1946 |
| Pensacola, FL | 75 | 49.3 | 42 | 92 | 87.3 | 78 | 1923 |
| Dauphin Is., AL | 69 | 46.4 | 45 | 91 | 86.8 | 77 | 1966 |
| Galveston, TX | 66 | 46.4 | 44 | 92 | 87.9 | 80 | 1957 |
| Port Mansfield, TX | 72 | 53.1 | 48 | 88 | 85.7 | 78 | 1963 |
| Newport Beach, CA | 63 | 55.9 | 54 | 78 | 72.7 | 58 | 1955 |
| Los Angeles Harbor CA | 69 | 52.7 | 51 | 77 | 72.4 | 61 | 1923 |
| Avila Beach, CA | 63 | 51.2 | 46 | 70 | 64.6 | 54 | 1945 |
| Santa Monica, CA | 63 | 54.1 | 51 | 74 | 70.8 | 60 | 1945 |
| San Francisco, CA | 58 | 48.4 | 44 | 66 | 63.4 | 50 | 1921 |
| San Francisco, CA | 59 | 49.5 | 47 | 68 | 62.1 | 56 | 1855[3] |
| Crescent City, CA | 57 | 46.0 | 44 | 65 | 61.1 | 48 | 1933 |
| Astoria, OR | 50 | 36.0 | 32 | 75 | 71.6 | 58 | 1925 |
| Neah Bay, WA | 51 | 42.2 | 38 | 62 | 55.8 | 47 | 1935 |
| Port Townsend, WA | 48 | 40.1 | 39 | 56 | 54.4 | 45 | 1973 |
| Seattle, WA | 51 | 43.7 | 42 | 64 | 59.1 | 52 | 1922 |

[4] See footnotes on previous page

# III  WATER QUALITY

   The quality of coastal water is important to us even if we can't drink
it, because we swim in it, harvest shellfish from it, and live near it.  We
have degraded coastal water quality by dumping sewage, discharging chemical
wastes, and spilling oil and other toxic substances into it.  These contaminants are taken up and concentrated in the body tissue of shellfish and
juvenile fishes and require the closing of shellfishing areas.  They spoil
our beaches and erode the beauty of the coast.
   The statistics presented in this section outline the character and
magnitude of water quality problems; for example, the ability of some
organisms to concentrate elements by two-million fold, the extent of
ocean dumpings, closings of shellfish beds, and characteristics of oil
spills.

# 14. SHELLFISH WATERS

The National Shellfish Register compiles information from state agencies on the status of the states' shellfish beds.  In this classification, open waters are waters that are approved for the direct market harvesting of shellfish.  These waters are below designated hazardous levels of pathogenic microorganisms and/or industrial wastes, as determined by sanitary survey.  Conditional waters are normally open waters subject to periodic closures. Restricted waters may be harvested if the shellfish are moved to open waters and allowed to purge themselves of contaminants.  Closed waters are closed to all shellfishing because of the current or probable future occurrence of hazardous levels of contaminants.  Most often, these contaminants are bacteria from sewage discharges.

The Pacific Coast states -- California, Oregon, and Washington -- have the highest percentage of closed waters (60.6% of the acreage classified here). Pennsylvania through Virginia have the lowest percentage -- 8.7%.  Note though that not all waters are classified here.

Table 14.  CONDITION OF SHELLFISH WATERS (ACRES), 1974.

| State | Open | Conditional | Restricted | Closed |
|-------|------|-------------|------------|--------|
| Maine | 930,325 | 6,531 | 6,728 | 101,281 |
| New Hampshire | | | | |
| Massachusetts | 310,881 | 325 | 4,091 | 29,060 |
| Rhode Island | 96,019 | 10,836 | | 20,134 |
| Connecticut | 248,751 | 2,227 | | 68,956 |
| Subtotal | 1,585,976 | 19,929 | 10,819 | 219,431 |
| New York | 477,241 | 266 | | 151,096 |
| New Jersey | 244,695 | 7,544 | 23,370 | 119,581 |
| Subtotal | 721,936 | 7,810 | 23,370 | 270,677 |
| Pennsylvania | | | | |
| Delaware | 205,153 | 153 | | 28,251 |
| Maryland | 1,213,576 | | | 111,319 |
| Virginia | 1,315,209 | 724 | | 120,271 |
| Subtotal | 2,733,938 | 877 | | 259,841 |
| North Carolina | 1,379,563 | | | 604,038 |
| South Carolina | 199,323 | 1,344 | | 74,917 |
| Georgia | 49,494 | | | 154,473 |
| Florida | 663,126 | 84,099 | | 1,024,966 |
| Alabama | 81,937 | 187,513 | | 85,589 |
| Mississippi | 76,232 | | | 27,678 |
| Subtotal | 2,449,675 | 272,956 | | 1,971,661 |
| Louisiana | 2,000,117 | | | 464,161 |
| Texas | 822,447 | | | 285,168 |
| Subtotal | 2,822,564 | | | 749,329 |
| California | 11,178 | 4,718 | | 263,045 |
| Oregon | 7,075 | 7,693 | | 13,305 |
| Washington | 155,655 | 21,313 | | 42,382 |
| Subtotal | 173,908 | 33,724 | | 318,732 |
| Grand Totals | 10,487,997 | 335,296 | 34,189 | 3,789,671 |

Source:  U.S. Environmental Protection Agency, Office of Enforcement, "National Shellfish Register of Classified Estuarine Waters-1974," EPA-330/1-75-002 (Denver, Colorado, December, 1975), p. 17.

# 15. BIOCONCENTRATION

Some marine organisms are filter feeders, and filter large volumes of water as they feed, extracting nutrients. In the process of filtering or contacting this water they concentrate certain elements, sometimes to an extraordinary degree. A scallop, for example, can concentrate cadmium by over 2 million times. In other words, a scallop may have a concentration of cadmium in its body 2 million times higher than the surrounding water. Phytoplankton are small plants that float in the upper layers of the ocean. They too concentrate certain elements, and these elevated concentrations may be passed on to the numerous animals that feed on the phytoplankton.

The levels concentrated in shellfish or other biota can potentially be used as an indicator of recent average levels of an element or a pollutant in seawater. Bioconcentration is also important to human health because food species may concentrate pollutants to a level harmful to humans that eat them.

Table 15a.  BIOCENCENTRATION OF METALS BY SHELLFISH.

Enrichment factors

|  | Scallop | Oyster | Mussel |
|---|---|---|---|
| Silver | 2,300 | 18,700 | 330 |
| Cadmium | 2,260,000 | 318,000 | 100,000 |
| Chromium | 200,000 | 60,000 | 320,000 |
| Copper | 3,000 | 13,700 | 3,000 |
| Iron | 291,500 | 68,200 | 196,000 |
| Manganese | 55,500 | 4,000 | 13,500 |
| Molybdenum | 90 | 30 | 60 |
| Nickel | 12,000 | 4,000 | 14,000 |
| Lead | 5,300 | 3,300 | 4,000 |
| Vanadium | 4,500 | 1,500 | 2,500 |
| Zinc | 28,000 | 110,300 | 9,100 |

Source:  R.R. Brooks and M.G. Rumsby. 1965. The Biochemistry of Trace Element Uptake by some New Zealand Bivalves. Limology and Oceanography 10:521-527.

Table 15b.   BIOCENCENTRATION OF METALS BY PHYTOPLANKTON.

| Element | Enrichment Factor | Element | Enrichment Factor |
|---------|-------------------|---------|-------------------|
| Aluminum | 10,000 | Manganese | 4,000 |
| Beryllium | 1,000 | Nickel | 5,000 |
| Cerium | 90,000 | Niobium | 1,000 |
| Chromium | 2,000 | Plutonium | 2,600 |
| Cobalt | 1,000 | Scandium | 2,000 |
| Copper | 30,000 | Silver | 20,000 |
| Iron | 40,000 | Zinc | 20,000 |
| Lead | 40,000 | Zirconium | 60,000 |

Source:   F.G. Lowman, et al.; 1971.   In Radioactivity in the Marine
Environment", National Academy of Sciences, Washington.
p. 161 In P.G. Brewer, 1975.   Minor Elements in Sea Water
In Chemical Oceanography. [eds.] J.P. Riley and G. Skirrow
Academic Press, N.Y., p. 430.

# 16. BIOCONTAMINATION

Given that some marine organisms concentrate various compounds, their
use as monitoring tools is enticing.   They sample water continuously and for
long periods without cost.   Dr. Edward Goldberg at the Scripps Institution
of Oceanography and others have capitalized on this feature in their "Mussel
Watch" program.   They have established 100 sampling location around the
country, and collect mussels or oysters at intervals.   Here, we identify
"hot spots," or locations where levels of contaminants were higher than
those sampled elsewhere for the sampled species.   Note that oysters are
usually more effective bioaccumalators than mussels.[1]

[1] Phillip Butler, pers. comm.

Table 16a.  BIOCONTAMINATION -- MUSSEL WATCH HOT SPOTS

| Location | Contaminant | Cause |
|---|---|---|
| | HEAVY METALS | |
| South San Francisco Bay | Silver 2.3 ppm[2] | |
| Savannah River, and | Silver 2.1-4.3 ppm | |
| Charleston, South Carolina[4] | Nickel 3.3-4.2 ppm | |
| | Zinc 2660-4060 ppm | |
| | Copper 192-220 ppm | |
| | Cadmium 2.7-3.7 ppm | |
| New York to New Hampshire | Cadmium 1.2 to 6.2 ppm | |
| | Copper 4.3 to 11 ppm | |
| Lake Sabine, Louisiana[4] | Copper 410 ppm | |
| | Zinc 7080 ppm | |
| | Silver 6.0 ppm | |
| | HALOGENATED HYDROCARBONS | |
| San Francisco to San Diego especially San Pedro | DDE[1] 17,000 ppb[3] DDD[1] 1,200 ppb | historical sewage outfall from manufacturing which is now discontinued |
| South San Francisco Bay, California | PCB 590 ppb | Numerous industrial sources |
| Rincon Point, California | PCB 130 ppb | |
| Point Fermin, California | PCB 250 ppb | |
| San Pedro Harbor, California | PCB 440-8700 ppb | |
| San Diego Harbor, California | PCB 360-1400 ppb | |
| Boston to New York | PCB to 838 ppb | |
| St. Augustine, Florida | PCB 149 ppb | |
| Narragansett Bay, Rhode Island | PCB 281-626 ppb | |
| | PETROLEUM HYDROCARBONS | |
| Espirito Santo Bay, Texas[4] | Contained aromatic compounds | |
| Matagorda Bay, Texas[4] | characteristic of petroleum | |
| Galveston Bay, Texas[4] | and which are not natural | |
| Boundary Bay, Washington | constituents of organisms | |

---

[1] Breakdown product of DDT, a biocide.  [2] ppm is parts per million (1 ppm equals one millionth of a gram per gram of organism dry weight).  [3] ppb is parts per billion (1 ppb equals one billionth of a gram per gram of organism dry weight).  [4] oysters, all others are mussels.
Source: E.D. Goldberg, et al. 1978.  The Mussel Watch Environmental Conservation, 5(2):1-25.

Fishes contact compounds in seawater either via their gills, from their food, or by transmission from their parents. If a compound is fat soluble, fishes can store it, and so fish too are useful monitoring tools. Information on three chlorinated hydrocarbons is presented here. PCB's are used as insulators in electric devices. They are no longer manufactured. DDT and Dieldrin are now in restricted use in the U.S.; they are both long-lived pesticides.

Connecticut, California, and Maryland rank highest in the percentage of samples with PCB, DDT, and Dieldrin residues respectively. Washington state, Delaware, and Georgia rank highest in the average concentration of residues (in those samples with residues) of PCB, DDT, and Dieldrin respectively.

Table 16b.  BIOCONTAMINATION -- THE OCCURRENCE OF BIOCIDE RESIDUES IN JUVENILE ESTUARINE FISHES BY STATE -- 1972-1976.

| | PCB | | DDT | | DIELDRIN | | |
|---|---|---|---|---|---|---|---|
| | % samples with residues | Average concentration[1] | % samples with residues | Average concentration[1] | % samples with residues | Average concentration | No. of Estuaries sampled |
| Rhode Island | 75 | 330 | 28 | 21 | -- | -- | 1 |
| Connecticut | 87 | 323 | 31 | 41 | 8 | 15 | 4 |
| New York | 63 | 262 | 72 | 76 | 4 | 24 | 3 |
| Delaware | 51 | 780 | 75 | 213 | 4 | 59 | 3 |
| Maryland | 36 | 306 | 58 | 108 | 25 | 30 | 8 |
| Virginia | 38 | 439 | 67 | 64 | 4 | 10 | 3 |
| North Carolina | 9 | 242 | 48 | 36 | 2 | 20 | 19 |
| South Carolina | 1 | 182 | 29 | 19 | -- | -- | 6 |
| Georgia | 3 | 323 | 10 | 22 | 3 | 60 | 9 |
| Florida | 26 | 83 | 52 | 24 | 18 | 10 | 11 |
| Alabama | 23 | 163 | 69 | 35 | -- | -- | 3 |
| Mississippi | 0 | -- | 29 | 75 | 10 | 17 | 4 |
| Louisiana | 2 | 256 | 12 | 38 | 2 | 15 | 14 |
| Texas | 24 | 135 | 67 | 49 | 12 | 20 | 9 |
| California | 31 | 229 | 87 | 77 | 2 | 34 | 7 |
| Oregon | 10 | 182 | 26 | 24 | -- | -- | 5 |
| Washington | 17 | 1674 | 4 | 23 | -- | -- | 6 |

[1] The arithmetic average in parts per billion of geometric means of positive samples in all collection years.

Source:  P.A. Butler and R.I. Schutzmann. 1978. Residues of Pesticides and PCB's in Estuarine Fish, 1972-76 - National Pesticide Monitoring Program. Pesticides Monitoring Journal, 12(2):51-59.

# 17. OCEAN DISPOSAL

Many of the Nation's most difficult waste disposal problems have been solved by ocean dumping, an activity that has been a source of controversy for the last 10 years.  The greatest trouble has been over the practice of New York City to dump sewage sludge in the shallow waters offshore from Sandy Hook, New Jersey.  This sludge has blighted an area of many square miles of ocean bottom displacing marine bottom life and has occasionally washed up on Long Island beaches where it has been termed "black mayonnaise" because of its appearance and consistency.

Table 17.  TYPES AND AMOUNT OF OCEAN DISPOSAL BY GEOGRAPHIC AREA (IN APPROX. TONS) -- 1973-1978.

| WASTE TYPE | 1973 | 1974 | (A)<br>1975 | ATLANTIC<br>1976 | 1977 | 1978 |
|---|---|---|---|---|---|---|
| Industrial Waste | 3,642,000 | 3,642,000 | 3,322,300 | 2,633,200 | 1,783,600 | 2,548,000* |
| Sewage Sludge | 4,898,900 | 5,010,000 | 5,039,600 | 5,134,000 | 5,270,900 | 5,535,000** |
| Construction and<br>Demolition Debris | 973,700 | 770,400 | 395,900 | 314,600 | 379,000 | 241,000 |
| Solid Waste | 0 | 0 | 0 | 0 | <100 | 0 |
| Explosives | 0 | 0 | 0 | 0 | 0 | 0 |
| Incinerated<br>(Wood) | 10,800 | 15,800 | 6,200 | 8,700 | 15,100 | 18,000 |
| Incinerated<br>(Chemicals) | 0 | 0 | 0 | 0 | 0 | 0 |
| TOTALS | 9,526,200 | 9,438,200 | 8,764,000 | 8,227,400 | 7,311,700 | 8,342,000 |

\* 1978 increase over 1977 due to plant shut down during a strike in 1976-77 at NL industries (a permittee).

\*\* 1978 increase primarily due to upgrading of sewage treatment plants to secondary treatment in NYC, Middlesex Co. and Joint Mtg. of Essex & Union Cos.

| WASTE TYPE | 1973 | 1974 | (B)<br>1975 | GULF<br>1976 | 1977 | 1978 |
|---|---|---|---|---|---|---|
| Industrial Waste | 1,408,000 | 937,700 | 119,600 | 100,300 | 60,200 | 173 |
| Sewage Sludge | 0 | 0 | 0 | 0 | 0 | 0 |
| Construction and<br>Demolition Debris | 0 | 0 | 0 | 0 | 0 | 0 |
| Solid Waste | 0 | 0 | 0 | 0 | 0 | 0 |
| Explosives | 0 | 0 | 0 | 0 | 0 | 0 |
| Incinerated<br>(Wood) | 0 | 0 | 0 | 0 | 0 | 0 |
| Incinerated<br>(Chemicals) | 0 | 12,300 | 4,100 | 0 | 17,600 | 0 |
| TOTALS | 1,408,000 | 950,000 | 123,700 | 100,300 | 77,800 | 173 |

| WASTE TYPE | | | (C) | PACIFIC | | |
|---|---|---|---|---|---|---|
| | 1973 | 1974 | 1975 | 1976 | 1977 | 1978 |
| Industrial Waste | 0 | 0 | 0 | 0 | 0 | 0 |
| Sewage Sludge | 0 | 0 | 0 | 0 | 0 | 0 |
| Construction and Demolition Debris | 0 | 0 | 0 | 0 | 0 | 0 |
| Solid Waste | 240 | 200 | 0 | 0 | 0 | 0 |
| Explosives | 0 | 0 | 0 | 0 | 0 | 0 |
| Incinerated (Wood) | 0 | 0 | 0 | 0 | 0 | 0 |
| Incinerated (Chemicals) | 0 | 0 | 0 | 0 | 12,100 | 0 |
| TOTALS | 240 | 200 | 0 | 0 | 12,100 | 0 |

| WASTE TYPE | TOTALS OF A, B, AND C | | | | | |
|---|---|---|---|---|---|---|
| | 1973 | 1974 | 1975 | 1976 | 1977 | 1978 |
| Industrial Waste | 5,050,800 | 4,579,700 | 3,441,900 | 2,733,500 | 1,843,800 | 2,548,173 |
| Sewage Sludge | 4,808,900 | 5,010,000 | 5,039,600 | 5,270,900 | 5,134,000 | 5,535,000 |
| Construction and Demolition Debris | 973,700 | 770,440 | 395,900 | 314,600 | 379,000 | 0 |
| Solid Waste | 240 | 200 | 0 | 0 | <100 | 0 |
| Explosives | 0 | 0 | 0 | 0 | 0 | 0 |
| Incinerated (Wood) | 10,800 | 15,800 | 6,200 | 8,700 | 15,100 | 18,000 |
| Incinerated (Chemicals) | 0 | 12,300 | 4,100 | 0 | 29,700 | 0 |
| TOTAL | 10,934,440 | 10,388,400 | 8,887,700 | 8,327,700 | 7,401,600 | 8,101,173 |

Source: Environmental Protection Agency, Office of Waste Water Programs. June 1979. Annual Report to Congress January-December 1978, Washington, D.C.

44

# 18. OIL SPILLS

The Federal Water Pollution Control Act requires that any discharge of oil or hazardous substance in harmful quantities, be reported to the "appropriate agency of the United States Government."  The Coast Guard has been designated as that agency by Executive Order 11735.  Tables 18a to 18h summarize some of the information that has been reported to the Coast Guard. Table 18i reports hydrocarbon spills during outer continental shelf activities (including pipeline spills, production spills, and spills from collisions) in the Gulf of Mexico.  Table 18b is derived from the U.S. Geological Survey.

The Coast Guard not only records coastal spills, but also spills on inland waters.  In some cases it has been possible to exclude inland spills from the data reported here.  Tables 18d, f, e and i detail information which is applicable only to coastal waters.  In the other cases, although the absolute numbers would change if it were possible to eliminate inland spills, the rank and the percentage of particular events quite probably would not.

These tables show that while most spills are small in volume, a very few large spills contribute most of the spilled volume.  Most spillage occurs on the Gulf Coast (numbers and volume), in ports and harbors (by number), and far offshore by volume.  The leading source of spills is classified "unknown" or "miscellaneous" (by number) and is "hull or tank rupture or leak" (by volume). The largest volume per spill is associated with pipelines, while offshore production and miscellaneous or unknown sources have the smallest volume per spill.

Table 18a.  OIL SPILLS BY YEAR REPORTED BY THE UNITED STATES COAST GUARD -- 1972-1977.[1]

| Year | Thousands of Gallons | Number of Spills |
|------|---------------------|------------------|
| 1972 | 16,764 | 8,380 |
| 1973 | 20,481 | 11,003 |
| 1974 | 16,916 | 11,435 |
| 1975 | 14,967 | 10,141 |
| 1976 | 23,125 | 10,660 |
| 1977 | 17,623[5] | 10,620[5] |

DISTRIBUTION OF OIL SPILLS BY NUMBER AND BY VOLUME CALENDAR YEAR 1976

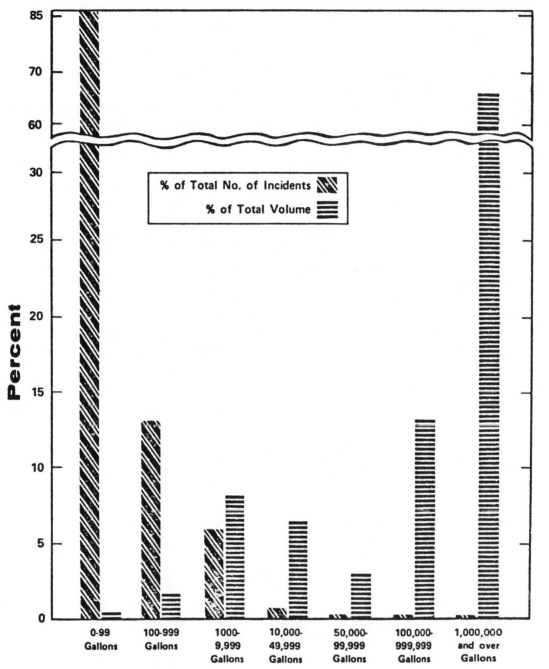

Examining the total number of oil spills reveals that the overwhelming majority are small.  On the other hand, when one examines the volume of oil spills, one finds that the majority of the volume spilled comes from a few very large spills. (Figure from U.S. Coast Guard. 1977, Polluting Incidents in and around U.S. Waters: Calendar Year 1976.)

Table 18b.  OIL SPILLS REPORTED DURING OUTER CONTINENTAL SHELF OPERATIONS
IN THE GULF OF MEXICO.[2]

| | Spills of 50 Bbl. or More | | | Spills of Less Than 50 Bbl. | |
|---|---|---|---|---|---|
| | Number | Barrels Spilled | | Number | Barrels Spilled |
| Year | | Largest | Total | | |
| 1970 | 7 | 53,000 | 84,325 | -- | -- |
| 1971 | 11 | 450 | 1,285 | 1,245 | 1,493 |
| 1972 | 2 | 100 | 150 | 1,159 | 1,032 |
| 1973 | 4 | 9,935 | 22,175 | 1,171 | 921 |
| 1974 | 8 | 19,833 | 22,721 | 1,129 | 667 |
| 1975 | 2 | 166 | 266 | 1,126 | 711 |
| 1976 | 3 | 4,000 | 4,714 | 948 | 522 |
| 1977 | 4 | 300 | 670 | 864 | 611 |
| 1978 | 3 | 900 | 1,139 | 873 | 581 |
| TOTAL | 44 | -- | 137,445 | 8,515 | 6,538 |

Total Spilled   143,983 barrels or 6,047,286 gallons

Table 18c.  OIL SPILLS BY COAST -- 1975-1977.[1]

| Coast | Number of Spills | % | Gallons Spilled | % |
|---|---|---|---|---|
| Atlantic | 7,322 | 31 | 11,981,278 | 31 |
| Gulf | 10,575 | 45 | 14,930,794 | 39 |
| Pacific | 5,397[5] | 23 | 11,625,877[5] | 30 |
| TOTAL | 23,294 | 100 | 38,537,949 | 100 |

Table 18d.  OIL SPILLS BY LOCATION -- 1976 and 1977.[1]

| | Number of Spills | % | Gallons Spilled | % |
|---|---|---|---|---|
| River Channels | 3,305 | 21 | 2,816,468 | 9 |
| Ports and Harbors | 6,649 | 43 | 3,058,634 | 10 |
| Beaches & Nonnavigable Waters | 888 | 6 | 6,880,809 | 22 |
| 0 to 3 miles offshore | 3,386 | 22 | 1,072,631 | 3 |
| 3 to 12 miles offshore | 703 | 5 | 47,500 | * |
| 12 miles + offshore | 692[5] | 4 | 17,325,083[5] | 56 |
| TOTALS | 15,590 | 100 | 31,201,125 | 100 |

Table 18e. OIL SPILLS BY COAST AND LOCATION -- 1976 and 1977.[1]

| | Number of Spills | Pct. | Volume of Spills (Gallons) | Pct. | Gallons Per Spill |
|---|---|---|---|---|---|
| **Atlantic** | | | | | |
| Total | 4,627 | | 10,515,589 | | 2,273 |
| River Channels | 1,457 | 31 | 829,559 | 8 | 569 |
| Ports & Harbors | 2,336 | 50 | 1,194,674 | 11 | 511 |
| Beaches & Nonnavigable Waters | 340 | 7 | 517,149 | 5 | 1,521 |
| 0 to 3 miles offshore | 403 | 9 | 404,361 | 4 | 1,003 |
| 3 to 12 miles offshore | 81 | 2 | 12,667 | * | 156 |
| 12 + miles offshore | 43 | * | 7,557,179 | 72 | 175,748 |
| **Pacific** | | | | | |
| Total | 3,629 | | 11,184,954 | | 3,082 |
| River Channels | 422 | 12 | 96,236 | * | 228 |
| Ports & Harbors | 2,275 | 63 | 1,149,484 | 10 | 505 |
| Beaches & Nonnavigable Waters | 223 | 6 | 243,778 | 2 | 1,093 |
| 0 to 3 miles offshore | 688 | 19 | 86,500 | * | 126 |
| 3 to 12 miles offshore | 64 | 2 | 4,175 | * | 65 |
| 12 + miles offshore | 31 | * | 9,604,781[3] | 86 | 309,832 |
| **Gulf** | | | | | |
| Total | 7,260 | | 9,500,582 | | 1,309 |
| River Channels | 1,426 | 20 | 1,890,673 | 20 | 1,326 |
| Ports & Harbors | 2,038 | 28 | 714,476 | 8 | 351 |
| Beaches & Nonnavigable Waters | 325 | 4 | 6,119,882 | 64 | 18,830 |
| 0 to 3 miles offshore | 2,295 | 32 | 581,770 | 6 | 254 |
| 3 to 12 miles offshore | 558 | 8 | 30,658 | * | 55 |
| 12 + miles offshore | 618 | 9 | 163,123 | 2 | 264 |

48

THE WRECK OF THE <u>ARGO MERCHANT</u>. The Argo Merchant, a Liberian tanker, ran aground 28 miles southeast of Nantucket Island carrying 7.3 million gallons of heavy industrial fuel oil. This grounding occurred in December, 1976. (photo courtesy of U.S. Coast Guard)

Table 18f.  OIL SPILLS BY SOURCE (VOLUME AND NUMBER) -- 1975-1977.[1]

| Source | Number of Spills | % of Total Number | Volume of Spills (Gallons) | % of Total Volume | Gallons Per Spill |
|---|---|---|---|---|---|
| Vessels | 9,679 | 31[5] | 28,871,528[5] | 52 | 2,982 |
| Land Vehicles | 1,215 | 4 | 1,941,003 | 4 | 1,598 |
| Non Transportation Facilities | 4,385 | 14 | 12,100,987 | 2 | 2,759 |
| Offshore Production | 3,639 | 12 | 433,546 | 1 | 119 |
| Pipelines | 1,672 | 5 | 9,350,683 | 17 | 5,592 |
| Marine Facilities | 1,609 | 5 | 879,593 | 2 | 547 |
| Land Facilities | 505 | 2 | 640,593 | 1 | 1,269 |
| Misc. or Unknown | 8,717 | 28 | 970,586 | 2 | 111 |
| TOTAL | 31,421 | 100 | 55,188,519 | 100 | 1,756 |

Table 18g.  OIL SPILLS BY LEADING CAUSES (VOLUME) -- 1975-1977.[1]

| Cause[4] | Gallons Spilled |
|---|---|
| Hull/Tank Rupture/Leak | 25,876,701[5] |
| Other Structural Failure | 10,614,536 |
| Pipe Rupture/Leak | 6,912,916 |
| Transportation Pipeline Rupture/Leak | 3,123,443 |
| Unknown/Miscellaneous | 1,397,778 |
| Tank Overflow | 1,110,311 |
| Other Equipment Failure | 1,077,496 |
| Other Personnel Error | 864,088 |
| Improper Handling Operation | 798,088 |
| Valve Failure | 741,103 |

Table 18h.  OIL SPILLS BY LEADING CAUSES (NUMBER) -- 1975-1977.[1]

| Cause | Number of Spills |
|---|---|
| Unknown/Miscellaneous | 10,632 |
| Other Equipment Failure | 2,792 |
| Tank Overflow | 2,534 |
| Pipe Rupture/Leak | 2,402 |
| Hull/Tank Rupture/Leak | 2,375[5] |
| Improper Handling Operation | 1,625 |
| Other Personnel Error | 1,433 |
| Transportation Pipeline Rupture/Leak | 1,308 |
| Other Structural Failure | 1,284 |
| Valve Failure | 1,008 |

---

* less than 1%

Source:   [1]U.S. Department of Transportation, U.S. Coast Guard.  1978.
Polluting Incidents in and around U.S. Waters: Calendar Year
1977 30 pp.; _____ 1977, Calendar Year
1976 31 pp.; _____ 1976, Calendar Year
1975.  24 pp.

[2]U.S. Department of Interior, Geological Survey-Conservation
Division.  1979.  Outer Continental Shelf Statistics Calendar
Year 1978.

[3]Excludes one spill of 9.6 million gallons in international
waters off Hawaii.

[4]Railroad/Highway/Aircraft Accidents were the cause of 1,495,129
gallons of oil spill in 1976 and 1977.  It was not reported as a
cause in 1975.

[5]Includes one 9.6 million gallon spill from the Hawaiian
Patriot spill that did not reach the U.S. 200 mile limit.

51

PELICANS RECOVER FROM OIL SPILL. These birds were soaked with oil by the wreck of the <u>Ocean</u> <u>Eagle</u> in San Juan harbor, Puerto Rico. (photo courtesy of U.S. Coast Guard by CPHOT John Lehman, U.S.C.G.)

# IV COUNTY PROFILES

People, cities, and businesses are attracted to the U.S. coast. Currently, 27 percent of our population, and 28 percent of our businesses are in coastal counties. Yet only 6 percent of our land area is in the coastal counties. The coast supports less agriculture than one might expect -- 4% of our farms are in coastal counties.

These tables describe, state by state, the amount of employment and business, farms and farm acreage, and metropolitan and non-metropolitan population in the coastal counties of each state. The selection of counties as "coastal" is somewhat arbitrary because the terms for selection vary greatly according to the purposes of the compiler. Our criteria for designation and our list of coastal counties are given in Table 19 and its accompanying text. These counties define the land portion of the coast.

# 19. COASTAL COUNTIES

Large amounts of statistical information are available for individual whole counties but very little for coastal parts of the counties, separately. The best that one can do for most of the data sets is to treat all counties that touch on coastal waters as coastal entities. Thus, one must first identify counties that one considers to be coastal and compile a list for each state. Because some coastal counties have large areas far from coastal waters this procedure will err slightly by including some areas which are not coastal. In states that have no large rivers (e.g., Maine, New Hampshire, and Alabama) this is a simple task. But states with large rivers (e.g., New York, Virginia, and Oregon) present a more difficult problem, because one must decide how far up the rivers to go. The list of coastal counties that we present is one which includes counties which we find to have substantial shoreline along, or physical interactions with saline waters. As with any list of coastal counties, ours is somewhat arbitrary. The reader will find that this list of coastal counties is shorter than many and could be categorized as a list of "maritime counties." Tables 20, 21, 22, 23 and 51 are based on this list of coastal counties.

Table 19.   COASTAL COUNTIES -- NAMES AND 1976 POPULATION.

| Alabama | | Florida | |
|---|---|---|---|
| Baldwin | 69,600 | Bay | 90,200 |
| Mobile* | 344,300 | Brevard | 231,400 |
| 67 Counties | | Broward* | 850,200 |
| 2 Coastal Counties | | Charlotte | 42,800 |
| | | Citrus | 38,300 |
| California | | Collier | 64,100 |
| Alameda* | 1,097,100 | Dade* | 1,438,500 |
| Contra Costa* | 598,700 | Dixie | 6,600 |
| Del Norte | 15,900 | Duval* | 556,500 |
| Humboldt | 105,900 | Escambia* | 226,500 |
| Los Angeles*, [1] | 7,003,800 | Flagler | 7,500 |
| Marin* | 221,400 | Franklin | 7,700 |
| Mendocino | 59,100 | Gulf* | 10,400 |
| Monterey | 271,500 | Hernando | 30,000 |
| Napa | 91,400 | Hillsborough* | 581,500 |
| Orange* | 1,755,600 | Indian River | 45,500 |
| San Diego* | 1,616,500 | Lee | 159,600 |
| San Francisco* | 663,600 | Levy | 16,600 |
| San Luis Obispo | 131,600 | Manatee | 123,700 |
| San Mateo* | 584,100 | Martin | 46,800 |
| Santa Barbara* | 284,200 | Monroe | 50,100 |
| Santa Clara* | 1,194,600 | Nassau | 29,900 |
| Santa Cruz | 162,900 | Okaloosa | 103,600 |
| Solano* | 193,800 | Palm Beach* | 466,200 |
| Sonoma | 255,200 | Pasco | 137,100 |
| Ventura | 450,900 | Pinellas* | 646,200 |
| 58 Counties | | St. Johns | 39,800 |
| 20 Coastal Counties | | St. Lucie | 69,300 |
| | | Santa Rosa* | 48,100 |
| Connecticut | | Sarasota | 162,600 |
| Fairfield* | 800,200 | Taylor | 14,200 |
| Middlesex | 125,200 | Volusia | 209,500 |
| New Haven* | 759,400 | Wakulla | 9,000 |
| New London | 243,900 | Walton | 17,700 |
| 8 Counties | | 67 Counties | |
| 4 Coastal Counties | | 34 Coastal Counties | |
| | | | |
| Delaware | | Georgia | |
| Kent | 91,900 | Bryan | 8,300 |
| New Castle* | 400,400 | Camden | 11,900 |
| Sussex | 89,600 | Charlton | 6,600 |
| 3 Counties | | Chatham* | 188,000 |
| 3 Coastal Counties | | Glynn | 48,900 |

55

Table 19.  COASTAL COUNTIES -- NAMES AND 1976 POPULATION (cont.).

Georgia (cont.)
  Liberty                    23,800
  McIntosh                    8,300
    159 Counties
    1 Consolidated Government
    7 Coastal Counties

Louisiana
  Cameron                     9,100
  Iberia                     62,700
  Jefferson*                413,400
  Lafourche                  74,800
  Orleans*                  564,100
  Plaquemines                26,300
  St. Bernard*               60,100
  St. Charles                33,300
  St. John the Baptist       25,900
  St. Mary                   61,600
  St. Tammany                81,900
  Tangipahoa                 73,000
  Terrebone                  85,800
  Vermillion                 45,300
  Washington                 42,900
    64 Parishes
    15 Coastal Parishes

Maine
  Cumberland*               204,400
  Hancock                    39,400
  Knox                       32,400
  Lincoln                    23,800
  Sagadohoc                  26,100
  Waldo                      27,000
    16 Counties
    8 Coastal Counties

Maryland
  Anne Arundel*             350,000
  Baltimore*                642,300
  Calvert                    28,000
  Cecil                      55,200
  Charles                    62,500
  Dorchester                 30,200
  Harford                   140,200

Maryland (cont.)
  Kent                       16,700
  Queen Annes                21,600
  St. Marys                  52,500
  Somerset                   19,800
  Talbot                     25,800
  Wicomico                   59,600
  Worcester                  27,200
    23 Counties
    14 Coastal Counties
  Baltimore City*           818,600
    1 Independent City
    1 Coastal Independent City

Massachusetts
  Barnstable                132,800
  Bristol*                  469,300
  Dukes                       7,800
  Essex*                    627,800
  Nantucket                   5,500
  Norfolk*                  618,200
  Plymouth*                 380,700
  Suffolk*                  714,400
    14 Counties
    8 Coastal Counties

Mississippi
  Hancock                    19,100
  Harrison                  145,500
  Jackson                   110,900
    82 Counties
    3 Coastal Counties

New Hampshire
  Rockingham                166,600
    10 Counties
    1 Coastal County

New Jersey
  Atlantic*                 190,600
  Bergen*                   878,400
  Cape May                   74,700
  Cumberland                132,400
  Hudson*                   574,100

56

Table 19.  COASTAL COUNTIES -- NAMES AND 1976 POPULATION (cont.).

| New Jersey (cont.) | | Oregon | |
|---|---|---|---|
| Middlesex | 592,300 | Clatsop | 39,200 |
| Monmouth | 490,500 | Columbia | 32,400 |
| Ocean | 305,600 | Coos | 60,100 |
| Salem* | 62,600 | Curry | 14,400 |
| Union* | 517,000 | Douglas | 82,800 |
| 21 Counties | | Lane* | 242,800 |
| 10 Coastal Counties | | Lincoln | 28,100 |
| | | Tillamook | 18,600 |
| New York | | 36 Counties | |
| Bronx* | 1,329,200 | 8 Coastal Counties | |
| Kings*,[2] | 2,381,600 | | |
| Nassau* | 1,404,400 | Rhode Island | |
| New York* | 1,407,100 | Bristol* | 45,700 |
| Queens* | 1,968,900 | Kent* | 149,700 |
| Richmond* | 328,800 | Newport | 81,700 |
| Rockland* | 254,300 | Providence* | 572,100 |
| Suffolk* | 127,500 | Washington | 86,500 |
| Westchester* | 879,300 | 5 Counties | |
| 62 Counties | | 5 Coastal Counties | |
| 9 Coastal Counties | | | |
| | | South Carolina | |
| North Carolina | | Beaufort | 60,100 |
| Beaufort | 39,900 | Charleston* | 263,000 |
| Bertie | 20,900 | Colleton | 29,500 |
| Brunswick | 32,900 | Georgetown | 38,200 |
| Camden | 5,700 | Horry | 88,900 |
| Carteret | 36,400 | Jasper | 13,200 |
| Chowan | 11,500 | 46 Counties | |
| Craven | 69,100 | 6 Coastal Counties | |
| Currituck | 10,200 | | |
| Dare | 9,600 | Texas | |
| Hyde | 5,700 | Aransas | 10,800 |
| New Hanover | 95,900 | Brazoria | 130,700 |
| Onslow | 115,100 | Calhoun | 17,800 |
| Pamlico | 9,600 | Cameron | 174,200 |
| Pasquotank | 28,300 | Chambers | 13,300 |
| Pender | 21,000 | Galveston* | 189,800 |
| Perquimans | 8,700 | Harris* | 2,067,900 |
| Tyrell | 3,900 | Jackson | 12,900 |
| Washington | 14,900 | Jefferson | 245,200 |
| 100 Counties | | Kenedy[4] | 600 |
| 18 Coastal Counties | | Kleberg | 33,000 |

Table 19.  COASTAL COUNTIES -- NAMES AND 1976 POPULATION (cont.)

Texas (cont.)

| | |
|---|---|
| Matagorda | 29,000 |
| Nueces* | 251,900 |
| Refugio | 9,100 |
| San Patricio | 51,300 |
| Willacy | 16,800 |
| 254 Counties | |
| 16 Coastal Counties | |

Virginia

| | |
|---|---|
| Accomack | 31,200 |
| Caroline | 16,300 |
| Charles City | 6,500 |
| Essex | 8,000 |
| Gloucester | 17,100 |
| Isle of Wight | 20,100 |
| James City | 20,900 |
| King and Queen | 6,000 |
| King George | 9,500 |
| King William | 8,200 |
| Lancaster | 9,800 |
| Mathews | 8,100 |
| Middlesex | 7,000 |
| New Kent | 7,300 |
| Northampton | 15,400 |
| Northumberland | 9,600 |
| Prince George | 20,800 |
| Richmond | 6,600 |
| Surry | 6,000 |
| Westmoreland | 13,400 |
| York* | 31,300 |
| 95 Counties | |
| 21 Coastal Counties | |

Virginia (cont.)

| | |
|---|---|
| Chesapeake* | 108,100 |
| Hampton* | 126,700 |
| Hopewell | 23,900 |
| Newport News* | 142,100 |
| Norfolk* | 284,100 |
| Portsmouth* | 108,600 |
| Suffolk | 46,400 |
| Virginia Beach* | 224,200 |
| Williamsburg | 11,600 |
| 38 Independent Cities | |
| 9 Coastal Independent Cities | |

Washington

| | |
|---|---|
| Clallam | 42,300 |
| Grays Harbor | 61,600 |
| Island | 36,400 |
| Jefferson | 12,400 |
| King* | 1,148,100 |
| Mason | 24,400 |
| Pacific | 16,000 |
| Pierce* | 420,800 |
| San Juan | 5,600 |
| Skagit | 55,800 |
| Snohomish* | 269,500 |
| Thurston | 97,200 |
| Wahkiakum | 3,700 |
| Whatcom | 91,500 |
| 39 Counties | |
| 14 Coastal Counties | |

---

* Metropolitan county
[1] Most populous coastal county
[2] Second most populous coastal county
[3] Second least populous coastal county
[4] Least populous coastal county
Source:  Adapted from U.S. Department of Commerce, Bureau of the Census.
         1977.  Current Population Reports, Series P-25.

# 20. AGRICULTURE

Coastal regions, especially the coastal plain from New Jersey through Texas, provide large flat areas that are amenable to agriculture. Agriculture effects coastal waters because the fertilizers, herbicides, and pesticides necessary for agriculture most easily enter coastal waters when applied in coastal counties. In addition, agriculture has historically impacted coastal resources by converting wetlands to agricultural purposes. As with any use of the land, agriculture changes the natural land forms and characteristics. For these reasons agricultural activity is important to coastal managers.

Table 20.  AGRICULTURE IN COASTAL COUNTIES.

| State | No. of Farms[1] | % of Farms[2] | Farm Acreage[1] | % of Acreage[2] | % of area in Farms[1] | Acres[3] | Acres[4] |
|---|---|---|---|---|---|---|---|
| Maine | 2,226 | 34.6 | 437,713 | 28.7 | 8.8 | 196.6 | 236.7 |
| New Hampshire | 372 | 15.0 | 45,829 | 9.0 | 10.4 | 123.2 | 210.0 |
| Massachusetts | 1,662 | 37.0 | 174,981 | 29.1 | 10.2 | 105.3 | 133.8 |
| Rhode Island | 597 | 100.0 | 61,068 | 100.0 | 9.1 | 102.3 | 102.3 |
| Connecticut | 1,356 | 39.6 | 151,867 | 34.5 | 10.4 | 112.0 | 128.6 |
| New York | 1,066 | 2.4 | 66,904 | 0.7 | 4.9 | 62.8 | 215.4 |
| New Jersey | 2,929 | 39.5 | 344,317 | 35.8 | 15.4 | 117.6 | 129.8 |
| Delaware | 3,400 | 100.0 | 630,605 | 100.0 | 49.7 | 185.5 | 185.5 |
| Maryland | 8,473 | 56.0 | 1,489,238 | 57.0 | 35.7 | 175.8 | 173.7 |
| Virginia | 5,150 | 9.7 | 1,207,571 | 12.5 | 26.7 | 234.5 | 183.7 |
| North Carolina | 8,193 | 9.0 | 1,321,727 | 11.8 | 23.9 | 161.3 | 123.2 |
| South Carolina | 3,947 | 13.5 | 802,029 | 13.0 | 24.2 | 203.2 | 211.0 |
| Georgia | 534 | 1.0 | 168,965 | 1.2 | 7.1 | 316.4 | 252.7 |
| Florida | 13,010 | 40.1 | 5,098,284 | 38.6 | 27.7 | 391.9 | 406.6 |
| Alabama | 2,109 | 3.7 | 406,832 | 3.4 | 22.6 | 192.9 | 209.1 |
| Mississippi | 685 | 1.3 | 110,507 | 0.8 | 9.6 | 161.3 | 266.7 |
| Louisiana | 5,800 | 17.0 | 1,589,947 | 17.0 | 21.9 | 274.1 | 274.8 |
| Texas | 8,923 | 5.1 | 6,654,449 | 5.0 | 74.5 | 745.8 | 770.9 |
| California | 21,147 | 31.2 | 9,431,361 | 28.2 | 41.2 | 446.0 | 493.3 |
| Oregon | 4,995 | 18.7 | 1,177,533 | 6.5 | 11.2 | 235.7 | 681.8 |
| Washington | 7,597 | 25.8 | 698,346 | 4.2 | 5.9 | 91.9 | 566.5 |
| | | | | | | | |
| Total Coastal Counties | 104,171 | 15.0 | 32,070,073 | 10.3 | 27.4 | 307.9 | 448.3 |
| Coastal States | 696,128 | 100.0 | 312,105,501 | 100.0 | (116,844,291)[5] | | |
| All U.S. | 2,314,013 | | 1,017,030,357 | | 44.9 | | 439.5 |

---

[1] Coastal
[2] Coastal as a percentage of the state
[3] Per coastal farm
[4] Per farm
[5] Total coastal county area in acres
Source:  Adapted from Q.S. Department of Commerce.  Bureau of the Census. Census of Agriculture: 1974.

# 21a. EMPLOYMENT AND BUSINESS

Business is attracted to the coast for many reasons, among them: access to bulk transportation facilities and marine resources. Based on our list of coastal counties (Table 19), 28 percent of all American businesses and employees are located in the coast. Outside of the completely coastal states (Rhode Island and Delaware), California has the greatest proportion of its businesses and employees in coastal counties (more than 75 percent), while North Carolina and Georgia have the lowest proportion of their businesses and employees in the coast (about 6 percent).

Table 21a. EMPLOYMENT AND BUSINESS ESTABLISHMENTS.

| State | Coastal Employees (in 100's)[1] | % of State Total | Coastal Businesses (in 100's)[1] | % of State Total |
|---|---|---|---|---|
| Maine | 1,270 | 47 | 115 | 51 |
| New Hampshire | 335 | 14 | 33 | 18 |
| Massachusetts | 5,988 | 32 | 422 | 38 |
| Rhode Island | 2,920 | 100 | 202 | 100 |
| Connecticut | 6,080 | 60 | 392 | 63 |
| New York | 37,532 | 68 | 2,473 | 68 |
| New Jersey | 11,735 | 53 | 759 | 54 |
| Delaware | 1,904 | 100 | 111 | 100 |
| Maryland | 6,056 | 56 | 364 | 53 |
| Virginia | 3,180 | 24 | 219 | 25 |
| North Carolina | 1,032 | 6 | 87 | 9 |
| South Carolina | 1,172 | 14 | 96 | 19 |
| Georgia | 878 | 6 | 60 | 6 |
| Florida | 13,140 | 56 | 1,036 | 58 |
| Alabama | 1,078 | 12 | 76 | 12 |
| Mississippi | 741 | 14 | 44 | 11 |
| Louisiana | 4,878 | 49 | 302 | 44 |
| Texas | 12,158 | 32 | 658 | 26 |
| California | 53,512 | 85 | 3,419 | 79 |
| Oregon | 1,201 | 19 | 116 | 22 |
| Washington | 6,460 | 69 | 498 | 65 |
| | | | | |
| All Coastal States | 177,141 | 63.8 | 11,675 | 61.6 |
| United States | 626,478 | 28.3[2] | 41,428 | 28.2[2] |

---

[1] As of March 12, 1976

[2] % of nation's employees or businesses in coastal counties

Source: U.S. Department of Commerce, Bureau of the Census, County Business Patterns: 1976.

SAN FRANCISCO, CALIFORNIA FROM 50,000 FEET. Of the states which are not entirely coastal, California has the highest proportion of its employees and businesses in the coastal counties. This is an infrared view of California taken by a U-2 aircraft in part of a NASA effort to analyze earth resources. (photo courtesy of NASA)

# 21. POPULATION CHARACTERISTICS

Many of our largest cities are in coastal counties, and so it is not surprising that a large fraction of the American public lives in this narrow strip. This population makes demands for living space, recreation, and waste disposal, and these demands must be met largely within the coastal counties and waters.

We break coastal population into population living in metropolitan (as determined by the Bureau of the Census), and non-metropolitan counties. This division reveals a number of interesting trends. Between 1960 and 1970, population growth in the coast exceeded that in the rest of the nation by 58 percent. Between 1970 and 1976, however, population growth in the coast trailed population growth in the nation by 32 percent. These tables show that this trend is the result of decreases in population in the metropolitan areas of the Northeast, and the Mid-Atlantic. Coastal non-metropolitan counties have, since 1960, outstripped national growth.

We find that 27.1 percent of all Americans lived in coastal counties in 1976. The Department of Commerce (Bureau of the Census, Statistical Abstract of the United States, 1979) concludes that 53 percent of the 1976 population of the United States was coastal. The difference arises from two sources. First, we do not include counties around the Great Lakes. Excluding the Great Lakes from the Commerce figures would leave 39 percent of the population in the coast. The remaining difference arises from our differences in defining coastal counties. Theirs includes any county or independent city entirely or substantially within 50 miles of U.S. coastal shorelines, whereas ours included only those that touch on saline waters. Therefore, our county list is shorter (see Table 19). By any measure, many Americans live in the narrow strip of land that constitutes the U.S. coast.

Table 21b.  COASTAL COUNTY POPULATION BY STATE -- 1960, 1970, 1976.

| State | 1960 | 1970 | 1976 | % Change In the Coast 60-70 | 70-76 | % Change In the State 60-70 | 70-76 |
|---|---|---|---|---|---|---|---|
| Maine | 439,851 | 464,883 | 509,700 | 5.7 | 9.6 | 2.4 | 8.0 |
| New Hampshire | 99,029 | 138,951 | 166,600 | 40.3 | 19.9 | 21.5 | 12.1 |
| Massachusetts | 2,597,027 | 2,862,093 | 2,956,500 | 10.2 | 3.3 | 10.5 | 1.8 |
| Rhode Island | 859,488 | 949,723 | 936,000 | 10.5 | -1.1 | 10.1 | -1.1 |
| Connecticut | 1,588,514 | 1,882,926 | 1,928,700 | 18.5 | 2.4 | 19.6 | 2.3 |
| New York | 10,694,633 | 11,574,982 | 10,081,100 | 8.2 | -12.9 | 8.7 | -1.0 |
| New Jersey | 3,146,738 | 3,718,552 | 3,818,200 | 18.2 | 2.7 | 18.2 | 2.6 |
| Delaware | 446,292 | 548,104 | 581,900 | 22.8 | 6.2 | 22.8 | 6.2 |
| Maryland | 2,026,229 | 2,293,907 | 2,350,200 | 13.2 | 2.5 | 26.5 | 5.2 |
| Virginia* | 688,158 | 1,327,372 | 1,356,400 | 92.9 | 2.2 | 17.2 | 8.7 |
| North Carolina | 441,605 | 477,404 | 538,400 | 8.1 | 12.8 | 11.5 | 7.5 |
| South Carolina | 403,667 | 441,785 | 492,900 | 9.4 | 11.6 | 8.7 | 9.8 |
| Georgia | 272,618 | 286,837 | 295,800 | 5.2 | 3.1 | 16.4 | 8.6 |
| Florida | 3,776,208 | 5,379,329 | 6,577,400 | 42.5 | 22.3 | 37.1 | 23.0 |
| Alabama | 363,389 | 376,690 | 413,900 | 3.7 | 9.9 | 5.4 | 6.1 |
| Mississippi | 189,050 | 239,944 | 275,500 | 26.9 | 14.8 | 1.8 | 6.7 |
| Louisiana | 1,335,181 | 1,546,663 | 1,660,200 | 15.8 | 7.3 | 11.8 | 6.4 |
| Texas | 2,258,833 | 2,828,725 | 3,254,300 | 25.2 | 15.0 | 16.9 | 12.5 |
| California | 12,320,082 | 15,724,192 | 16,757,800 | 27.6 | 6.6 | 27.0 | 0.1 |
| Oregon | 393,635 | 455,570 | 508,400 | 15.7 | 11.6 | 18.2 | 11.5 |
| Washington | 1,756,506 | 2,220,278 | 2,284,800 | 26.4 | 2.9 | 19.5 | 0.1 |
| | | | | | | | |
| Total Coastal | 46,096,733 | 55,738,910 | 57,744,700 | 20.9 | 3.6 | 16.8 | 5.2 |
| National[1] Total | 179,108,000 | 202,728,000 | 213,377,000 | --- | --- | 13.2[2] | 5.3[2] |
| % Coastal | 25.7 | 27.5 | 27.1 | --- | --- | --- | --- |
| Coastal States | 94,936,612 | 110,925,225 | 116,741,069 | --- | --- | --- | --- |

Table 21c.   COASTAL COUNTY NONMETROPOLITAN POPULATION BY STATE -- 1960, 1970, 1976.

| | | | | % Change | |
|---|---|---|---|---|---|
| State | 1960 | 1970 | 1976 | 1960-1970 | 1970-1976 |
| Maine | 257,100 | 272,355 | 305,300 | 5.9 | 12.1 |
| New Hampshire | 99,029 | 138,951 | 166,600 | 40.3 | 19.9 |
| Massachusetts | 79,674 | 106,547 | 146,100 | 33.7 | 37.1 |
| Rhode Island | 140,945 | 179,934 | 168,200 | 27.7 | -6.5 |
| Connecticut | 274,610 | 345,164 | 369,100 | 25.7 | 6.9 |
| New York | 0 | 0 | 0 | -- | -- |
| New Jersey | 1,031,903 | 1,435,060 | 1,595,500 | 39.1 | 11.2 |
| Delaware | 138,846 | 162,248 | 181,500 | 16.9 | 11.9 |
| Maryland | 388,143 | 469,667 | 539,300 | 21.0 | 14.8 |
| Virginia* | 271,284 | 331,142 | 331,300 | 22.1 | 0.0 |
| North Carolina | 441,605 | 477,404 | 538,400 | 8.1 | 12.8 |
| South Carolina | 187,285 | 194,135 | 229,900 | 3.7 | 18.4 |
| Georgia | 84,319 | 99,021 | 107,800 | 17.4 | 8.9 |
| Florida | 897,869 | 1,358,150 | 1,811,800 | 51.3 | 33.4 |
| Alabama | 49,088 | 59,382 | 69,600 | 21.0 | 17.2 |
| Mississippi | 189,050 | 239,944 | 275,500 | 26.9 | 14.8 |
| Louisiana | 466,701 | 564,439 | 622,600 | 20.9 | 10.3 |
| Texas | 653,738 | 679,457 | 744,700 | 3.9 | 9.6 |
| California | 949,739 | 1,305,379 | 1,544,400 | 37.4 | 18.3 |
| Oregon | 230,745 | 242,212 | 265,600 | 5.0 | 9.7 |
| Washington | 327,703 | 387,382 | 446,400 | 18.2 | 15.2 |
| | | | | | |
| Total Coastal | 7,159,376 | 9,047,973 | 10,459,600 | 26.4 | 15.6 |
| National Total | 51,373,000 | 53,503,000 | 57,714,000 | 4.1[2] | 7.9[2] |
| % Coastal | 13.9 | 16.9 | 18.1 | | |

Table 21d.  COASTAL COUNTY METROPOLITAN POPULATION BY STATE -- 1960, 1970, 1976.

| State | 1960 | 1970 | 1976 | % Change 1960-1970 | % Change 1970-1976 |
|---|---|---|---|---|---|
| Maine | 182,751 | 192,528 | 204,400 | 5.4 | 6.2 |
| New Hampshire | 0 | 0 | 0 | -- | -- |
| Massachusetts | 2,517,353 | 2,755,546 | 2,810,400 | 9.5 | 2.0 |
| Rhode Island | 718,543 | 769,789 | 767,800 | 7.1 | -0.3 |
| Connecticut | 1,313,904 | 1,537,762 | 1,559,600 | 17.0 | 1.4 |
| New York | 10,694,633 | 11,574,982 | 10,081,100 | 8.2 | -12.9 |
| New Jersey | 2,114,835 | 2,283,492 | 2,222,700 | 8.0 | -2.7 |
| Delaware | 307,446 | 385,856 | 400,400 | 25.5 | 3.8 |
| Maryland | 1,638,086 | 1,824,240 | 1,810,900 | 11.4 | -0.7 |
| Virginia* | 416,874 | 996,230 | 1,025,100 | 139.0 | 2.9 |
| North Carolina | 0 | 0 | 0 | -- | -- |
| South Carolina | 216,382 | 247,650 | 263,000 | 14.5 | 6.2 |
| Georgia | 188,299 | 187,816 | 188,000 | -0.3 | 0.1 |
| Florida | 2,878,339 | 4,021,179 | 4,765,600 | 39.7 | 18.5 |
| Alabama | 314,301 | 317,308 | 344,300 | 1.0 | 8.5 |
| Mississippi | 0 | 0 | 0 | -- | -- |
| Louisiana | 868,480 | 982,224 | 1,037,600 | 13.1 | 5.6 |
| Texas | 1,605,095 | 2,149,268 | 2,509,600 | 33.9 | 16.8 |
| California | 11,370,343 | 14,418,813 | 15,213,400 | 26.8 | 5.5 |
| Oregon | 162,890 | 213,358 | 242,800 | 31.0 | 13.8 |
| Washington | 1,428,803 | 1,832,896 | 1,838,400 | 28.3 | 0.3 |
| | | | | | |
| Total Coastal | 38,937,357 | 46,690,937 | 47,285,100 | 19.9 | 1.3 |
| National Total[1] | 127,079,000 | 148,730,000 | 155,860,000 | 17.0[2] | 4.8[2] |
| % Coastal | 30.6 | 31.4 | 30.3 | | |

Table 21e.   COASTAL COUNTY POPULATION BY REGIONS -- 1960, 1970, 1976.

| | 1960 | 1970 | 1976 | % Change 1960-1970 | % Change 1970-1976 |
|---|---|---|---|---|---|
| | | All Coastal | Counties | | |
| Northeast[3] | 16,278,542 | 17,873,558 | 16,578,600 | 9.8 | -7.3 |
| Mid Atlantic[4] | 6,307,417 | 7,887,935 | 8,106,700 | 25.1 | 2.8 |
| South Atlantic[5] | 4,894,098 | 6,585,355 | 7,904,500 | 34.6 | 20.0 |
| Gulf | 4,146,453 | 4,992,022 | 5,603,900 | 20.4 | 12.3 |
| Pacific | 14,470,223 | 18,400,040 | 19,551,000 | 27.1 | 6.3 |
| | | Metropolitan | | | |
| Northeast | 15,427,184 | 16,830,607 | 15,423,300 | 9.1 | -8.4 |
| Mid Atlantic | 4,477,241 | 5,489,818 | 5,459,100 | 22.6 | -0.6 |
| South Atlantic | 3,283,020 | 4,456,645 | 5,216,600 | 35.8 | 17.1 |
| Gulf | 2,787,876 | 3,448,800 | 3,891,500 | 23.7 | 12.8 |
| Pacific | 12,962,036 | 16,465,067 | 17,294,600 | 27.0 | 5.0 |
| | | Nonmetropolitan | | | |
| Northeast | 851,358 | 1,042,951 | 1,155,300 | 22.5 | 10.8 |
| Mid Atlantic | 1,830,176 | 2,398,117 | 2,647,600 | 31.0 | 10.4 |
| South Atlantic | 1,611,078 | 2,128,710 | 2,687,900 | 32.1 | 26.3 |
| Gulf | 1,358,577 | 1,543,222 | 1,712,400 | 13.6 | 11.0 |
| Pacific | 1,508,187 | 1,934,973 | 2,256,400 | 28.3 | 16.6 |

* There were jurisdictional changes between 1960 and 1976
[1] Exclusive of Alaska and Hawaii
[2] % increase in the National Total
[3] Maine to New York
[4] New Jersey to Virginia
[5] North Carolina to Florida
[6] Alabama to Texas
[7] California to Washington
  Coastal States Totals (1970-110,925,225; 1976-116,741,069; 1960-94,936,612)
Source:   1960 and 1970 is adapted from U.S. Department of Commerce, Bureau
          of the Census, Census of Population: 1970, Vol. I, Part A;  1976
          is adapted from Department of Commerce, Bureau of the Census,
          Current Population Reports, Series P-25.

Table 21f.  COASTAL POPULATION CHARACTERISTICS BY STATE -- 1976.

| State | % of Population in Coastal Counties (1976) | % Nonmetro-politan (1976) | State | % of Population in Coastal Counties (1976) | % Nonmetro-politan (1976) |
|---|---|---|---|---|---|
| ME | 47.6 | 59.9 | SC | 17.3 | 46.6 |
| NH | 20.1 | 100.0 | GA | 5.9 | 36.4 |
| MA | 51.1 | 4.9 | FL | 78.8 | 27.5 |
| RI | 100.0 | 18.0 | AL | 11.3 | 16.8 |
| CT | 62.2 | 19.1 | MS | 11.6 | 100.0 |
| NY | 55.8 | 0.0 | LA | 42.8 | 37.5 |
| NJ | 51.9 | 41.8 | TX | 25.8 | 22.9 |
| DE | 100.0 | 31.2 | CA | 83.9 | 9.2 |
| MD | 57.0 | 22.9 | OR | 21.9 | 52.2 |
| VA | 26.8 | 24.4 | WA | 66.9 | 19.5 |
| NC | 9.9 | 100.0 | Total | | |
|  |  |  | Coastal | 49.5 | 18.1 |
|  |  |  | National | 27.1 | 37.0 |

POPULATION GROWTH OF PARTS OF THE NATION AS COMPARED TO THE NATION AS A WHOLE

67

POPULATION GROWTH OF PARTS OF THE NATION AS COMPARED TO THE NATION AS A WHOLE

Here, we compare the growth rate of parts of the United States to the nation as a whole.  The tic marks along the vertical axis mark growth rates 1% greater, and 1% less than annual national growth rate.  Note that a 2% annual growth rate (which is about the rate of the Nonmetropolitan coastal counties) means that the population will double in about 35 years.  The parts of the nation whose growth is shown here are:

A.  Coastal Counties (as listed in Table 19)
B.  Coastal States (as listed in Table 19)
C.  Nonmetropolitan coastal counties (as listed in Table 19)
D.  National nonmetropolitan counties
E.  Metropolitan coastal counties (as listed in Table 19)
F.  Metropolitan counties nationwide.

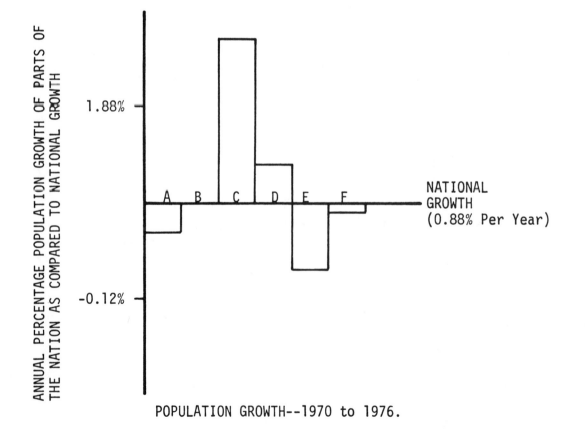

POPULATION GROWTH--1970 to 1976.

THE CHESAPEAKE BAY TO NEW YORK CITY FROM OUTER SPACE. This six photograph montage was taken from an Earth Resources Technology Satellite-1 (ERTS-1) at an altitude of 562 statute miles. Many notable geographic landmarks are obvious: The Barriers islands along the coast of New Jersey, and the Delmarva peninsula; the Susquehanna and Potomac Rivers flowing into the Chesapeake Bay; the Delaware river broadening out into the Delaware Bay; and the Appalachian Mountains of Pennsylvania. (photo courtesy of NASA)

# V  ENERGY

Energy is crucial for the functioning of our society.  Here, we describe state by state, the distribution of two types of energy resources in the coast.  First, in Table 22 and 23 we describe nuclear and nonnuclear electrical generating facilities which are located in the coast.  These facilities have requirements which the coast and coastal waters can meet.  However, they often negatively effect the environment in which they are located.  Estuarine locations, particularly, have a high potential for impacts.  Society will have to decide how to balance expected environmental costs against the benefits of coastal locations--keeping in mind the advantages and disadvantages of the alternatives.

Another form of energy which impacts the coast is the offshore production of gas and oil.  The quantities produced offshore are large.  In 1978, 13% of domestic crude oil, and 26% of domestic natural gas were produced offshore.  The acquisition of this energy has substantial potential to impact the coastal environment.

# 22. ELECTRICAL POWER

Given the demands of coastal population and business, energy generation in the coast is a necessity. Coastal counties, adjacent to enormous supplies of cooling water, provide the technological criteria essential to the installation of electrical generating facilities. This table lists all sources of electrical generating capacity -- nuclear, hydroelectric, coal, oil, gas and geyser. Each of these has its own peculiar effects on the coast. The information given here is based on the county list given in Table 19.

The Northeast and Mid-Atlantic regions have large amounts of capacity installed within the coastal counties (63 and 64% of the state totals respectively). The Gulf Coast (excluding Florida) has the lowest percentage of it capacity installed in coastal counties (26%). Georgia has the smallest percentage of its electrical generating capacity in the coast of any state with 7 percent of the total in coastal counties.

Note that because several plants are typically located at one site, the number of sites of electrical plants is considerably less than the number of plants.

THERMAL DISCHARGES from power plants unprotected by closed cycle cooling may cause heavy stress to estuarine ecosystems (Moss Landing, California) (Photo by John Clark)

Table 22. COASTAL ELECTRICAL GENERATING CAPACITY BY STATE (ALL SOURCES).

| State | Number of Plants | Capacity (Megawatts) | Percentage of States' Plants | Percentage of States' Capacity |
|---|---|---|---|---|
| Maine | 62 | 1,691 | 41 | 83 |
| New Hampshire | 10 | 635 | 22 | 41 |
| Massachusetts | 81 | 5,845 | 44 | 61 |
| Rhode Island | 8 | 249 | 100 | 100 |
| Connecticut | 53 | 5,751 | 61 | 93 |
| New York | 153 | 17,923 | 31 | 57 |
| New Jersey | 79 | 8,985 | 66 | 72 |
| Delaware | 23 | 1,632 | 100 | 100 |
| Maryland | 85 | 6,946 | 88 | 76 |
| Virginia | 41 | 3,937 | 38 | 38 |
| North Carolina | 17 | 2,671 | 10 | 17 |
| South Carolina | 27 | 2,288 | 14 | 19 |
| Georgia | 23 | 1,076 | 13 | 7 |
| Florida | 264 | 25,441 | 85 | 91 |
| Alabama | 10 | 1,950 | 7 | 11 |
| Mississippi | 9 | 1,797 | 25 | 33 |
| Louisiana | 45 | 6,043 | 37 | 48 |
| Texas | 98 | 12,489 | 27 | 25 |
| California | 208 | 26,205 | 38 | 70 |
| Oregon | 34 | 1,076 | 17 | 11 |
| Washington | 77 | 2,212 | 30 | 12 |
| | | | | |
| All Coastal | 1,407 | 136,842 | 37 | 45 |
| All United States[1] | 9,174 | 578,666 | 15[2] | 24[2] |
| Region | | | | |
| Northeast | 367 | 32,094 | 38 | 63 |
| Mid Atlantic | 228 | 21,500 | 65 | 64 |
| South Atlantic | 331 | 31,476 | 39 | 44 |
| Gulf | 162 | 22,279 | 24 | 26 |
| Pacific | 319 | 29,493 | 32 | 45 |

[1] Excluding Alaska and Hawaii
[2] Coastal county plants or capacity as a percentage of the nations total.
Source: Adapted from Kenneth J. Shanks. April, 1979. Inventory of Power Plants in the United States. U.S. Department of Energy, Office of Energy Data and Interpretation.

# 23. NUCLEAR POWER

The coast provides technologically feasible sites for nuclear power plants, because of the access to massive amounts of cooling water typical of the coast. We give the name and location of existing and projected nuclear power plants, along with figures on the capacity (in Megawatts = MW), the maximum ΔT (the maximum increase in temperature of the effluent water in °F), and the rate of water intake in cubic feet per second (cfs). A nuclear power plant is deemed coastal if it occurs in one of the coastal counties listed in Table 19. It may be instructive to compare these to the figures on temperature in Table 13, and river discharge in Table 10.

If construction proceeds as projected, 11 of 21 coastal states plan to increase the percentage of their electrical generating capacity based on coastal nuclear power. At present, Maine has the highest percentage of its capacity installed as coastal nuclear power with 42 percent.

Note that because several plants are typically located at one site, the number of sites of nuclear power plants is considerably less than the number of plants.

Table 23. NUCLEAR POWER PLANTS IN THE COASTAL ZONE.

| State | Location | Plant Name | MW | Max. ΔT | Intake (cfs) | Status | Coastal Nuclear Power and % of States Existing Capacity | Projected Capacity |
|---|---|---|---|---|---|---|---|---|
| ME | Wiscasset | Yankee | 864 | 25 | 950 | Op. | 42 | 32 |
| NH | Seabrook | Seabrook 1[b] | 2200 | 45 | 1733 | 12/82 | 0 | 57 |
| | | " 2[b] | | | | 12/84 | | |
| MA | Plymouth | Pilgrim 1 | 678 | 29 | 720 | Op. | | |
| | | " 2[c] | 1180 | | | 6/85 | 7 | 16 |
| RI | N. Kingston | Rome Pt. 1 | 2300 | | | 11/86 | 0 | 90 |
| | | " 2 | | | | 11/88 | | |
| CT | Haddam Neck | Haddam | 662 | 22 | 870 | Op. | 35 | 45 |
| | Waterford | Millstone 1 | 662 | 22 | 935 | Op. | | |
| | | " 2 | 910 | 23 | 1150 | Op. | | |
| | | " 3 | 1156 | | | 5/86 | 3 | |
| NY | Brookhaven | Shoreham | 844 | 20 | 1275 | 9/80 | 7 | 11 |
| | Buchanan | Indian Pt 1 | 275 | 15 | 695 | Op. | | |
| | | " 2 | 1013 | 15 | 1950 | Op. | | |
| | | " 3 | 1013 | 16 | 1920 | Op. | | |
| | Suffolk Co. | Jamesport 1[b] | 1191 | | | 7/88 | | |
| | | " 2[b] | 1191 | | | 7/90 | | |
| NJ | Lacey Twp. | Oyster Creek | 550 | 20 | 960 | Op. | 14 | 34 |
| | | Forked R.[b] | 1251 | | | 12/83 | | |
| | Salem | Salem 1 | 1170 | 14 | 5100 | Op. | | |
| | | " 2[a] | 1115 | | | 79 | | |
| | Salem Co. | Hope Creek 1[b] | 1067 | | | 9/84 | | |
| | | " 2[b] | 1067 | | | 5/86 | | |
| MD | Lusby | Calvert Cliffs 1 | 918 | 10 | 5490 | Op. | 20 | 13 |
| | | " 2 | 911 | | | Op. | | |
| VA | Williamsburg | Surry 1 | 847.5 | 14 | -- | Op. | 16 | 10 |
| | | " | 847.5 | | | Op. | | |
| NC | Southport | Brunswick 1 | 866.7 | 14 | 4000 | Op | 11 | 6 |
| | | " 2 | 866.7 | | | Op. | | |
| FL | Florida City | Turkey Pt 3 | 760 | 15 | -- | Op. | 12 | 11 |
| | | " 4 | 760 | | | Op. | | |
| | Fort Pierce | St. Lucie 1 | 850 | | | Op. | | |
| | | " 2[b] | 850 | | | 4/83 | | |
| | Crystal R. | Crystal R. 3 | 890 | 17 | 1520 | Op. | | |
| LA | St. Charles Co. | Waterford 3[a] | 1165 | | | 4/81 | 0 | 5 |
| TX | Matagorda Co. | South Tx. 1 | 1250 | | | 10/80 | 0 | 3 |
| | | " 2 | 1250 | | | 3/82 | | |
| CA | San Clemente | San Onofre 1 | 450 | 19 | 793 | Op. | 1 | 12 |
| | | " 2[a] | 1181 | 20 | 2213 | 11/81 | | |
| | | " 3[a] | 1181 | | | 11/83 | | |
| | Diablo Canyon | Diablo Canyon 1[a] | 1136 | 20 | 3684 | 79 | | |
| | | " 2[a] | 1159 | | | 79 | | |
| | | " 3 | 1181 | | | 1/83 | | |
| | Humbolt Bay | Humbolt Bay 3 | 65.3 | | | Op. | | |
| OR | Ranier | Trojan 1 | 1216.0 | | | Op. | 12 | 9 |
| WA | Grays Harbor | Satsop 1[b] | 1240 | | | 1/84 | | |
| | County | Satsop 2[b] | 1240 | | | 7/85 | 0 | 8 |

Source: Adapted from Kenneth J. Shanks. April, 1979. Inventory of Power Plants in the United States. U.S. Department of Energy, Office of Energy Data and Interpretation. John Clark and Willard Brownell, 1973. Electric Power Plants in the Coastal Zone: Environmental Issues. American Littoral Society Special Publication No. 7. Highlands, NJ. Plant Status, New York Times, Oct. 23, 1979, Page B7.

Footnotes
[a] operation Permit pending
[b] construction Permit pending
[c] construction Permit pending

# 24. OFFSHORE OIL AND GAS

Oil and gas are produced offshore in great quantities. In 1978 over 13 percent of domestically produced oil and over 26 percent of domestically produced natural gas came from offshore wells. Offshore waters have two divisions. The Outer Continental Shelf (OCS) includes shelf waters beyond state territorial waters. The OCS is under federal jurisdiction and has an area of 875,000 square miles. Oil and gas produced shoreward of the boundary are produced on state lands. In Texas and West Florida, the state lands extend 3 marine leagues offshore (about 10 miles), and everywhere else the state lands extend to only three miles offshore. The seaward limit of the OCS is not well defined legally, but extends roughly to include all submergd lands that lie under less than 200 meters of water (about 650 feet).

The U.S. Department of the Interior determines which areas will be bid upon. A bidder proposes some combination of royalties, and bonus for the right to drill for specified minerals. In addition, he is charged a rental fee which is set by the Department of the Interior. The U.S. Geological Survey, on the basis of exploratory findings selects that bid which it believes will produce the most revenue. Minimum royalties have been 16-2/3% of the production value of minerals taken from the lease. Annual rental and minimum royalty has been $3-10 per acre. A lease is typically about 5,000 acres. Through this bidding and royalty system, the federal government has received 70% of the total production value of the oil and gas produced on the OCS from 1953 through 1978. In some years, however, the revenue paid by the drilling companies to the federal government has been greater than the production value of the minerals, due to (among other reasons) large bonuses paid for the lease initially, compensated for by oil and gas obtained at a later date.

Most of the U.S. offshore (state and federal) oil and gas has been produced off the coast of Louisiana.

Note that some conversion factors pertaining to oil and gas may be found in Table 53f.

AN OIL PLATFORM in the Gulf of Mexico off Louisiana.  (photo courtesy
of U.S. Coast Guard)

Table 24a.  REVENUE AND PRODUCTION VALUE OF OUTER CONTINENTAL SHELF LEASES.

| Year | Total Revenue (in Thousand $) | Total Production Value (in Thousand $) | % Cumulative Revenue of Cumulative Production Value |
|------|------|------|------|
| 1953 | 2,358 | 5,037 | 47 |
| 1954 | 147,660 | 14,370 | 774 |
| 1955 | 117,197 | 27,061 | 575 |
| 1956 | 11,716 | 39,498 | 324 |
| 1957 | 14,840 | 61,073 | 200 |
| 1958 | 20,150 | 96,471 | 129 |
| 1959 | 118,829 | 150,473 | 110 |
| 1960 | 323,782 | 200,970 | 127 |
| 1961 | 51,345 | 273,636 | 93 |
| 1962 | 564,570 | 376,676 | 102 |
| 1963 | 98,963 | 450,866 | 87 |
| 1964 | 194,939 | 506,784 | 76 |
| 1965 | 146,445 | 594,223 | 65 |
| 1966 | 354,466 | 801,725 | 60 |
| 1967 | 675,859 | 947,215 | 63 |
| 1968 | 1,558,052 | 1,179,912 | 77 |
| 1969 | 362,029 | 1,443,870 | 66 |
| 1970 | 1,238,961 | 1,707,593 | 68 |
| 1971 | 456,012 | 2,135,677 | 59 |
| 1972 | 2,624,958 | 2,229,179 | 69 |
| 1973 | 3,494,981 | 2,486,865 | 80 |
| 1974 | 5,598,758 | 3,570,054 | 94 |
| 1975 | 1,723,325 | 3,924,915 | 86 |
| 1976 | 2,967,860 | 4,402,440 | 83 |
| 1977 | 2,509,742 | 5,774,056 | 76 |
| 1978 | 2,941,112 | 7,096,500 | 70 |
| TOTAL | 28,318,912 [1] | 40,497,138 [1] | 70 |

[1] Columns do not add to totals, because of rounding after addition.

77

Table 24b.   PRODUCING OUTER CONTINENTAL SHELF OIL AND GAS LEASES (BY YEAR AND ADJACENT STATE).

| | California | | Texas | | Louisiana | | Total | |
|------|-----|---------|-----|---------|-----|-----------|-----|------------|
| Year | No. | Acres | No. | Acres | No. | Acres | No. | Acres |
| 1954 | 0 | 0 | 0 | 0 | 58 | 240,028 | 58 | 240,028 |
| 1955 | 0 | 0 | 4 | 5,760 | 102 | 432,316 | 106 | 438,076 |
| 1960 | 0 | 0 | 13 | 23,040 | 285 | 1,141,959 | 298 | 1,164,999 |
| 1965 | 0 | 0 | 13 | 37,620 | 406 | 1,632,544 | 419 | 1,670,164 |
| 1970 | 10 | 42,256 | 34 | 146,340 | 557 | 2,329,365 | 601 | 25,117,961 |
| 1971 | 12 | 53,776 | 34 | 146,340 | 596 | 2,497,933 | 642 | 2,698,049 |
| 1972 | 16 | 76,816 | 39 | 166,320 | 636 | 2,659,880 | 691 | 2,903,016 |
| 1973 | 17 | 82,576 | 42 | 174,960 | 660 | 2,769,934 | 719 | 3,027,470 |
| 1974 | 29 | 145,012 | 44 | 186,480 | 668 | 2,803,654 | 741 | 3,135,146 |
| 1975 | 14 | 63,617 | 44 | 189,630 | 725 | 2,987,540 | 783 | 3,240,787 |
| 1976 | 14 | 63,617 | 70 | 330,414 | 749 | 3,082,564 | 833 | 3,476,595 |
| 1977 | 24 | 121,672 | 92 | 454,278 | 780 | 3,317,335 | 896 | 3,893,285 |
| 1978 | 24 | 121,672 | 121 | 615,583 | 786 | 3,366,831 | 931 | 4,104,086 |


Table 24c.   TOTAL OFFSHORE OIL PRODUCTION BY STATE THROUGH 1978.

| Adjacent State | State Lands Thousands of Barrels | % of State's Total Offshore | OCS Lands Thousands of Barrels | % of State's Total Offshore | State % of Total Offshore Prod. |
|----------------|------------|--------|------------|--------|--------|
| Alaska | 663,445 | 100 | 0 | 0 | 7.9 |
| California | 1,670,050 | 90 | 185,561 | 10 | 22.1 |
| Louisiana | 1,165,074 | 20 | 4,660,298 | 80 | 69.5 |
| Texas | 17,960 | 43 | 23,808 | 57 | 0.5 |

Table 24d.   TOTAL OFFSHORE GAS PRODUCTION BY STATE THROUGH 1978.

| Adjacent State | Millions of Cubic Feet | % of State's Total Offshore | Millions of Cubic Feet | % of State's Total Offshore | State % of Total Offshore Prod. |
|----------------|------------|--------|------------|--------|--------|
| Alaska | 733,690 | 100 | 0 | 0 | 1.4 |
| California | 628,737 | 90 | 69,860 | 10 | 1.4 |
| Louisiana | 8,786,472 | 19 | 37,458,119 | 81 | 90.5 |
| Texas | 1,825,685 | 53 | 1,619,004 | 47 | 6.7 |

THE OUTER CONTINENTAL SHELF. Spottail pinfish and gorgonians (soft coral) at a depth of about 100 feet 30 miles off the coast of North Carolina. This rock outcrop is an unusual "island" on the shelf off the Atlantic Coast (Photo by Mark Hooper).

Table 24e.  OFFSHORE PRODUCTION OF CRUDE OIL AND CONDENSATES BY YEAR.

| Year | Total U.S. Production (millions of barrels) | Total Offshore Production (millions of barrels) | % from OCS Lands | % from State Lands | % of Domestic Production from Offshore Sources |
|------|------|------|------|------|------|
| 1954 | 2,315 | 48.6 | 7 | 93 | 2.10 |
| 1955 | 2,484 | 59.1 | 11 | 89 | 2.38 |
| 1956 | 2,617 | 73.4 | 15 | 85 | 2.80 |
| 1957 | 2,617 | 83.7 | 19 | 81 | 3.20 |
| 1958 | 2,449 | 86.2 | 29 | 71 | 3.52 |
| 1959 | 2,575 | 100.1 | 36 | 64 | 3.89 |
| 1960 | 2,574 | 116.8 | 43 | 57 | 4.54 |
| 1961 | 2,622 | 133.4 | 48 | 52 | 5.09 |
| 1962 | 2,676 | 162.2 | 55 | 45 | 6.06 |
| 1963 | 2,753 | 188.1 | 56 | 44 | 6.83 |
| 1964 | 2,787 | 214.8 | 57 | 43 | 7.71 |
| 1965 | 2,849 | 242.7 | 60 | 40 | 8.52 |
| 1966 | 3,028 | 300.3 | 63 | 37 | 9.92 |
| 1967 | 3,216 | 368.2 | 60 | 40 | 11.45 |
| 1968 | 3,329 | 471.2 | 57 | 43 | 14.15 |
| 1969 | 3,372 | 525.8 | 59 | 41 | 15.59 |
| 1970 | 3,517 | 575.7 | 63 | 37 | 16.37 |
| 1971 | 3,454 | 615.1 | 68 | 32 | 17.81 |
| 1972 | 3,456 | 614.8 | 67 | 33 | 17.79 |
| 1973 | 3,361 | 582.7 | 68 | 32 | 17.34 |
| 1974 | 3,203 | 532.7 | 68 | 32 | 16.63 |
| 1975 | 3,057 | 495.3 | 67 | 33 | 16.20 |
| 1976 | 2,968 | 462.9 | 68 | 32 | 15.60 |
| 1977 | 2,985 | 438.7 | 69 | 31 | 14.70 |
| 1978 | 3,150 | 416.6 | 70 | 30 | 13.23 |
| 1954-1978 | 73,414 | 7,909.1 | 61 | 39 | 10.77 |

Table 24f.  OFFSHORE PRODUCTION OF NATURAL GAS BY YEAR.

| Year | Total U.S. Production (billions of cubic feet) | Total Offshore Production (billions of cubic feet) | % from OCS Lands | % from State Lands | % Offshore OCS & State |
|------|------|------|------|------|------|
| 1954 | 8,743 | 84.8 | 66 | 34 | 0.97 |
| 1955 | 9,405 | 128.2 | 63 | 37 | 1.36 |
| 1956 | 10,082 | 143.4 | 58 | 42 | 1.42 |
| 1957 | 10,680 | 174.3 | 47 | 53 | 1.63 |
| 1958 | 11,030 | 258.0 | 49 | 51 | 2.34 |
| 1959 | 11,620 | 353.4 | 59 | 41 | 3.04 |
| 1960 | 12,771 | 440.5 | 62 | 38 | 3.45 |
| 1961 | 13,254 | 478.1 | 67 | 33 | 3.61 |
| 1962 | 13,877 | 640.3 | 71 | 29 | 4.61 |
| 1963 | 14,667 | 763.3 | 74 | 26 | 5.20 |
| 1964 | 15,462 | 849.8 | 73 | 27 | 5.50 |
| 1965 | 16,040 | 939.4 | 69 | 31 | 5.86 |
| 1966 | 17,207 | 1,373.2 | 73 | 27 | 7.98 |
| 1967 | 18,171 | 1,837.8 | 65 | 35 | 10.11 |
| 1968 | 19,322 | 2,321.3 | 66 | 34 | 12.01 |
| 1969 | 20,698 | 2,844.7 | 69 | 31 | 13.74 |
| 1970 | 21,921 | 3,218.1 | 75 | 25 | 14.68 |
| 1971 | 22,493 | 3,750.7 | 74 | 26 | 16.67 |
| 1972 | 22,532 | 3,757.4 | 81 | 19 | 16.68 |
| 1973 | 22,647 | 3,975.3 | 83 | 17 | 17.55 |
| 1974 | 21,601 | 4,229.8 | 83 | 17 | 19.58 |
| 1975 | 20,109 | 4,257.5 | 81 | 19 | 21.17 |
| 1976 | 19,952 | 4,296.3 | 84 | 16 | 21.53 |
| 1977 | 20,025 | 4,540.0 | 82 | 18 | 22.67 |
| 1978 | 19,597 | 5,104.1 | 86 | 14 | 26.05 |
| 1954-1978 | 413,906 | 50,759.7 | 78 | 22 | 12.26 |

Source:  Adapted from U.S. Department of the Interior, Geological Survey-Conservation Division.  Outer Continental Shelf Statistics-Calendar Year 1978.

# VI ESTUARINE AND WETLAND RESOURCES.

"An estuary is a semi-enclosed coastal body of water which has a free connection with the open sea and within which sea water is measureably diluted with fresh water derived from land drainage."[1]  These areas are associated with tremendous primary and secondary productivity.  Many commercial and recreational fishes live in estuaries either for their entire lives, or for important parts of their lives.

Typically, estuaries are bordered by wetlands.  Coastal saline wetlands are areas that are subject to periodic immersion, and so their habitat, productivity, and other attributes are part of the marine environment.  It is widely believed that they are key parts of the marine environment.  Further, many terrestial species have coastal wetlands as a part of their habitat.

Estuaries lengthen the shoreline, and therefore provide points of access to the coastal waters for many people.

[1] Donald W. Pritchard.  1967.  "What is an estuary:  Physical Viewpoint."  In Estuaries, edited by George H. Lauff.  AAAS.  Washington, D.C.

# 25. ESTUARINE AREAS

The total area of coastal estuaries is over 15 million acres. This is about one-half of the area of the state of New York. In 1967 the U.S. Fish and Wildlife Service considered almost half of the estuarine area to be "important habitat" for fish and wildlife. In the twenty years preceding this report, the area of this important habitat had decreased by almost 8 percent. California experienced the greatest decrease as the San Francisco-Suisun Bay lost 192,000 out of 294,000 estuarine acres between 1950 and 1967 until filling was virtually stopped by state action. Maryland, Georgia, and Virginia each lost less than 1 percent of their important estuarine habitat in the years 1947 to 1967.

Table 25. FISH AND WILDLIFE ESTUARINE HABITAT LOST -- 1947-1967.

| | Acres of Estuaries | | |
| State | Total Area | Basic Area of Important Habitat | Area of Basic Habitat Lost by Dredging and Filling | Percent Loss of Habitat |
|---|---|---|---|---|
| Alabama | 530,000 | 132,800 | 2,000 | 1.5 |
| California | 552,100 | 381,900 | 255,800 | 67.0 |
| Connecticut | 31,600 | 20,300 | 2,100 | 10.3 |
| Delaware | 395,500 | 152,400 | 8,500 | 5.6 |
| Florida | 1,051,200 | 796,200 | 59,700 | 7.5 |
| Georgia | 170,800 | 125,000 | 800 | 0.6 |
| Louisiana | 3,545,100 | 2,076,900 | 65,400 | 3.1 |
| Maine | 39,400 | 15,300 | 1,000 | 6.5 |
| Maryland | 1,406,100 | 376,300 | 1,000 | 0.3 |
| Massachusetts | 207,000 | 31,000 | 2,000 | 6.5 |
| Mississippi | 251,200 | 76,300 | 1,700 | 2.2 |
| New Hampshire | 12,400 | 10,000 | 1,000 | 10.0 |
| New Jersey | 778,400 | 411,300 | 53,900 | 13.1 |
| New York | 376,600 | 132,500 | 19,800 | 15.0 |
| North Carolina | 2,206,600 | 793,700 | 8,000 | 1.0 |
| Oregon | 57,600 | 20,200 | 700 | 3.5 |
| Rhode Island | 94,700 | 14,700 | 900 | 6.1 |
| South Carolina | 427,900 | 269,400 | 4,300 | 1.6 |
| Texas | 1,344,000 | 328,100 | 68,100 | 8.2 |
| Virginia | 1,670,000 | 428,100 | 2,400 | 0.6 |
| Washington | 193,800 | 95,500 | 4,300 | 4.5 |
| TOTAL | 15,347,000 | 7,115,900 | 563,000 | 7.9 |

Source: Modified from U.S. Fish and Wildlife Service Tabulation, p. 30, hearings on estuarine areas, House Merchant Marine and Fisheries subcommittee on fisheries and wildlife conservation, March 6, 8, 9, 1967.

# 26. WETLAND TYPES AND LOSS

The Soil Conservation Service has estimated the original, natural wetlands of this country at 127 million acres.[1]

In 1956, the Interior Department published a wetlands survey, which was the product of state and federal investigations of portions of states. They classified wetlands into 20 types. Types 1 through 11 are noncoastal. The remainder are coastal and are defined in Table 27. These wetland types are, despite their shortcomings, now widely used although a new classification system has recently been developed by the Fish and Wildlife Service.[2]

Experienced wetland scientists have estimated the acreage of wetland types at various times in the past, and from these figures, gross wetland loss can be imprecisely determined. These figures can present a misleading picture of a very dynamic system, however. For example, it appears that mangroves (Type 20) have sustained no losses between 1954 and 1978. However, in 1954, the mangrove stands in the Florida Keys and Bay had been devastated by a series of hurricanes, and the inventory that year followed a succession of wet years. Between 1954 and 1978, there was revegetation of mangroves at some sites but considerable natural and man-induced losses at other locations, particularly the filling of mangrove swamps on the southwest Florida coast for housing developments. However, the digging of new drainage canals, the reopening of old canals, and the development of waterways for recreation craft has resulted in saline intrusion and the extension of the mangrove forest northward into the Everglades.[3] A very dynamic story is hidden behind two numbers. (R. Macomber, U.S. Army Corps of Engineers, pers. comm.)

[1] Wetlands of the United States. Circular 39, 1956.

[2] L.M. Cowardin, V. Carter, F.C. Golet, E.T. LaRoe, 1979. Classification of Wetlands and Deepwater Habitats of the United States. U.S. Department of the Interior, Fish and Wildlife Service, Office of Biological Services. 103 pp.

[3] The Trees of South Florida: The Natural Environments and Their Succession, Frank C. Craighead, Sr., 1971.

Table 26. EXISTING COASTAL WETLANDS AND WETLANDS LOSS BY TYPE -- 1780, 1954, 1978.

| Wetland Types | Existing Wetlands (millions of acres) | | | Acres of Wetland Lost Annually | |
|---|---|---|---|---|---|
| | 1780 | 1954 | 1978 | 1780 to 1954 | 1954 to 1978 |
| 12 to 14 | 6.0 | 4.0 | 2.0 | 11,500 | 83,000 |
| 15 to 18 | 4.5 | 3.7 | 3.2 | 4,800 | 20,800 |
| 20 | 0.5 | 0.5 | 0.5 | 0 | 0 |
| TOTAL | 11.0 | 8.2 | 5.7 | 10,300 | 103,800 |

Source: R. Macomber, U.S. Army Corps of Engineers, pers. comm.;

# 27. WETLAND TYPES

Table 27.  WETLAND TYPE DESCRIPTIONS.

| Type | Name | Water Depth | Dominant Plants |
|------|------|-------------|-----------------|
| 12 | Coastal shallow fresh[1] marshes | Up to 6 inches at high tide | Diverse freshwater and brackish species including many grasses, reeds, rushes and sedges |
| 13 | Coastal deep fresh marshes | Up to 3 feet at high tide | Diverse freshwater and brackish species |
| 14 | Coastal open freshwater | Up to depths of 10 feet | Pondweeds, milfoils, wildcelery, wigeongrass, and others |
| 15 | Coastal salt flats | A few inches at high tide | Glassworts, saltwort and seablite |
| 16 | Coastal salt meadows | A few inches at monthly high tide | Saltmeadow cordgrass, and saltgrass |
| 17 | Irregularly flooded salt marshes | Up to a few inches at times | Needlerush |
| 18 | Regularly flooded salt marshes | Up to 2 feet at daily high tide | Saltmarsh cordgrass |
| 20 | Mangrove swamps | Up to 2 feet | Mangroves (four species) |

[1] Includes low brackish estuaries where mean salinities are below 10%.
Source:  U.S. Department of the Interior.  Fish and Wildlife Service. 1971. Wetlands of the United States.  Their extent and their value to waterfowl and other wildlife. Circular 39.

SALT MARSH near Bogue Inlet, North Carolina (Photo by Mark Hooper).

# 28. WETLAND AREA

The 1954 wetlands survey of the U.S. Fish and Wildlife Service determined that there were over 7 million acres of coastal wetlands. Almost half of this area was in Louisiana. In general, the data for this survey were collected by examination of maps and field checks or by relying on the knowledge of local state and federal agents. These data generally exclude wetlands less than 40 acres in size.

Table 28. 1954 ESTIMATES OF COASTAL WETLANDS BY STATE AND TYPE

| State | Acres of Wetland Type | | | | |
|-------|-------|-------|-------|-------|-------|
| | 12&13 | 15&16 | 17 | 18 | Total |
| Maine[1] | 11,549 | 16,178 | --- | 1,455 | 29,182 |
| New Hampshire | 400 | 5,285 | --- | 375 | 6,060 |
| Massachusetts[1] | 3,435 | 34,520 | --- | 7,940 | 45,895 |
| Rhode Island | 195 | 1,360 | --- | 645 | 2,200 |
| Connecticut | 6,442 | 7,496 | --- | 2,037 | 15,975 |
| New York[1] | 9,010 | 24,855 | --- | 11,530 | 45,395 |
| New Jersey[1] | 69,750 | 150,440 | --- | 20,870 | 241,060 |
| Delaware | 20,714 | 49,578 | --- | 43,756 | 114,048 |
| Maryland | 70,330 | 64,790 | 53,050 | 15,890 | 204,060 |
| Virginia | --- | 20,250 | 24,700 | 86,100 | 210,250 |
| North Carolina | 47,500 | --- | 100,450 | 58,400 | 206,350 |
| South Carolina | 80,400 | --- | 91,000 | 345,000 | 516,400 |
| Georgia | 31,700 | 650 | 74,850 | 285,650 | 392,850 |
| Florida | 38,800 | 39,600 | 302,900 | 46,100<br>20-523,000 | 950,400 |
| Alabama | 17,350 | --- | 12,100 | --- | 29,450 |
| Mississippi | 28,463 | 1,758 | 5,790 | 18,398 | 54,409 |
| Louisiana | 2,951,262 | 33,000 | 15,400 | 520,800 | 3,520,462 |
| Texas | 44,114 | 528,053 | 18,378 | 18,888 | 609,433 |
| California | 10,730 | 23,497 | --- | 83,605 | 117,832 |
| Oregon | 10,250 | 1,125 | --- | 1,895 | 13,270 |
| Washington | --- | 8,340 | --- | 6,795 | 15,135 |
| TOTAL | 3,452,394 | 1,010,775 | 698,618 | 1,576,129 | 7,260,916 |

Source: [1]George P. Spinner. 1959. A plan for the marine resources of the Atlantic coastal zone. New York: American Geographical Society, remaining states from 1954 wetland surveys published by the U.S. Department of the Interior, U.S. Bureau of Sport Fisheries and Game.

# 29. WETLAND AREA

Since the 1954 wetlands survey of the U.S. Fish and Wildlife Service, many of the states have conducted their own surveys. These surveys were conducted for a variety of reasons, by a variety of methods, and used a variety of criteria. For example, some states surveyed every wetland, regardless of size, while others included only those over 40 acres in size. Because of this diversity, these results should not be compared to those in Table 28 for the purpose of determining changes in the area of wetland. Each state defined its own wetland types, and in order to list them together, we have superimposed the categories shown below. The "Salt to Brackish" category is a subdivision of the other two categories. The "All Coastal" and "All Tidal" categories are probably equivalent, and reflect each state's own designation. Louisiana has the greatest wetland acreage followed by Florida, Georgia, and Texas (in that order).

Table 29. MOST RECENT STATE ESTIMATES OF COASTAL WETLANDS (ACRES).

| State | Salt to Brackish | All Coastal | All Tidal |
|---|---|---|---|
| Maine | 16,909 | 28,303 | --- |
| New Hampshire | --- | --- | 7,500 |
| Massachusetts | 43,280 | --- | --- |
| Rhode Island | 3,668 | 15,635 | --- |
| Connecticut | --- | --- | 15,387 |
| New York | --- | --- | 23,500 |
| New Jersey | --- | --- | 245,000 |
| Delaware | 74,516 | 83,450 | --- |
| Maryland | 165,379 | 211,647 | --- |
| Virginia | 164,886 | --- | 212,874 |
| North Carolina | 158,850 | 206,350 | --- |
| South Carolina | 369,463 | 515,235 | --- |
| Georgia | --- | --- | 475,000 |
| Florida | 981,803 | 2,254,160 | --- |
| Alabama | 16,004 | 121,603 | --- |
| Mississippi | 63,982 | 64,805 | --- |
| Louisiana | 2,066,763 | 3,910,664 | --- |
| Texas | 374,912 | 412,516 | --- |
| California | --- | 126,000 | --- |
| Washington | --- | 15,135 | --- |
| Oregon | 18,823 | 29,933 | --- |
| TOTAL | 4,519,238 | 7,995,436 | 979,261 |

Coastal and Tidal                                                      8,974,697

**Source**

ME Frederick B. Hurley, pers. comm., Department of Inland Fisheries and Wildlife. Augusta, Maine.

NH C.H.J. Breeding, et. al., October, 1974. Soil Surveys of New Hampshire Tidal Marshes, University of New Hampshire Agricultural Experiment Station, Res. Rpt. No. 40.

MA W.P. MacConnell, 1975. Bulletin 630, Massachusetts Cooperative Extension Center, University of Massachusetts, Amherst.

RI W.P. MacConnell, 1974. Remote Sensing Land Use and Vegetative Cover in Rhode Island, Cooperative Extension Service, University of Rhode Island, Kingston.

CT Robert Leach, pers. comm., Connecticut Department of Environmental Protection.

NY John Ren Kavinsky, pers. comm., New York Department of Environmental Conservation, Division of Marine Resources, Tidal Wetlands Bureau.

NJ Thomas F. Hampton, undated memorandum, Properties Affected by the Wetlands order and Procedural Rules and Regulations. New Jersey Department of Environmental Protection, Division of Marine Resources, Trenton.

DE F.C. Darber, et. al., 1976. An Atlas of Delaware's Wetland and Estuarine Resources. Delaware Coastal Management Program, Technical Report No. 2.

MD Elder Ghigiarelli, pers. comm., Maryland Department of Natural Resources, Coastal Zone Unit, Annapolis.

VA Arthur F. Harris, pers. comm., Virginia Institute of Marine Science, Gloucester Point.

NC Kenneth A. Wilson, April, 1962. North Carolina Wetlands, Their Distribution and Management. North Carolina Wildlife Resources Comm., Raleigh.

SC Ralph W. Tiner, Jr., 1979. An Inventory of South Carolina's Coastal Marshes. South Carolina Wildlife and Marine Resources Department, Marine Resources Center, Charleston Technical Report No. 23.

GA Fred Marland, pers. comm., Georgia Department of Natural Resources, Marshland Protection Brunswick, Georgia.

FL Anonymous, March, 1978. Statistical Inventory of Key Biophysical Elements in Florida's Coastal Zone. Florida Department of Environmental Regulation, Division of Environmental Programs, Bureau of Coastal Zone Planning, Tallahassee.

AL B.A. Vittor and J.P. Stout, 1975. Delineation of Ecological Critical Areas in the Alabama Coastal Zone. Marine Environmental Science Consortium, Dauphin Island.

MS Lionel Electeris, 1973. The Marshes of Mississippi, pp. 147-190. In J.Y. Christmas [ed.] Cooperative Gulf of Mexico Inventory and Study, Mississippi.

LA William S. Perret, et. al., 1971. Cooperative Gulf of Mexico Estuarine Inventory and Study, Louisiana Phase I, Area Description. Louisiana Wildlife and Fisheries Commission.

TX John Batterton, pers. comm., Texas Bureau of Economic Geology.

CA Bruce M. Browning, pers. comm., California Department of Fish and Game, Coastal Wetlands Program, Sacramento.

OR G.J. Atkins and C.A. Jefferson, August 1973. Coastal Wetlands of Oregon. Oregon Coastal Conservation and Development Commission, Florence.

WA No recent data, information transferred from Table 28.

# 30. DREDGE AND FILL PERMITS AND VIOLATIONS

Based on records from October 1977 through September 1978, when a violation of federal dredge and fill law (Section 404 of the Clean Water Act) is reported, 28 percent of the projects receive an after-the-fact permit, 60 percent are found not to require a permit, and 12 percent are submitted for litigation. When an application is submitted, 16 percent are withdrawn or cancelled, and 1 percent are denied. Sometimes the applications are withdrawn or cancelled by the applicant, because "we work with the applicant and in some cases where issuance is unlikely we might 'discourage' the applicant from further processing because the permit would not likely be approved."[1] Therefore, the distinction between the withdrawn and denied categories is not as clear cut as it might be.

These data are based on the reports of coastal districts, which cover large areas. When we queried district offices as to the percentage of permits which were issued in either coastal or tidal waters, we were told that it was more than three quarters. Of the offices that were contacted, only the Mobile, Alabama district quoted a lower figure -- 35 percent.

These data are applicable to wetlands, because a portion of the dredging and filling takes place within wetlands. The Corps has no record of what this portion is.

[1] Pers. comm. Curtis L. Clark, U.S. Army Corps of Engineers. April, 1980.

Table 30a.  DREDGE & FILL PERMITS (A TO C) AND REPORTED VIOLATIONS (D TO G) FROM ALL COASTAL DISTRICTS.

| Action[1] | Section 10 Permits # | Section 10 Permits % | Section 404 Permits # | Section 404 Permits % | Section 10 & 404 Permits # | Section 10 & 404 Permits % | All Permits # | All Permits % |
|---|---|---|---|---|---|---|---|---|
| A | 857 | 14 | 279 | 22 | 951 | 18 | 2,087 | 16 |
| B | 52 | * | 19 | 2 | 84 | 2 | 155 | 1 |
| C | 5,436 | 86 | 958 | 76 | 4,241 | 80 | 10,635 | 83 |
| D | 297 | 32 | 71 | 17 | 212 | 29 | 580 | 28 |
| E | 535 | 57 | 297 | 72 | 422 | 57 | 1,254 | 60 |
| F | 104 | 11 | 44 | 11 | 107 | 14 | 255 | 12 |
| G | 936 | 100 | 412 | 100 | 741 | 100 | 2,082 | 100 |

Table 30b. DREDGE & FILL PERMITS (A TO C) AND REPORTED VIOLATIONS (D TO G) --
Districts New England and New York, New York

| Action[1] | Section 10 Permits | | Section 404 Permits | | Section 10 & 404 Permits | | All Permits | |
|---|---|---|---|---|---|---|---|---|
| | # | % | # | % | # | % | # | % |
| A | 76 | 16 | 23 | 10 | 172 | 31 | 271 | 21 |
| B | 5 | 1 | 2 | * | 10 | 2 | 17 | 1 |
| C | 400 | 83 | 215 | 90 | 378 | 68 | 993 | 78 |
| D | 70 | 32 | 8 | 47 | 81 | 38 | 159 | 35 |
| E | 86 | 39 | 9 | 53 | 93 | 43 | 188 | 41 |
| F | 65 | 29 | 0 | 0 | 42 | 19 | 107 | 24 |
| G | 221 | 100 | 17 | 100 | 216 | 100 | 454 | 100 |

Table 30c. DREDGE & FILL PERMITS (A TO C) AND REPORTED VIOLATIONS (D TO G) --
Districts Philadelphia, Pennsylvania through Savannah, Georgia

| Action[1] | Section 10 Permits | | Section 404 Permits | | Section 10 & 404 Permits | | All Permits | |
|---|---|---|---|---|---|---|---|---|
| | # | % | # | % | # | % | # | % |
| A | 187 | 12 | 86 | 21 | 374 | 23 | 647 | 18 |
| B | 22 | 1 | 9 | 2 | 37 | 2 | 68 | 2 |
| C | 1,383 | 87 | 315 | 77 | 1,228 | 75 | 2,926 | 80 |
| D | 101 | 48 | 32 | 17 | 87 | 30 | 220 | 32 |
| E | 107 | 50 | 131 | 71 | 187 | 64 | 425 | 62 |
| F | 4 | 2 | 21 | 11 | 19 | 6 | 44 | 6 |
| G | 212 | 100 | 184 | 100 | 293 | 100 | 689 | 100 |

Table 30d. DREDGE & FILL PERMITS (A TO C) AND REPORTED VIOLATIONS (D TO G) --
Districts Jacksonville, Florida through Galveston, Texas

| Action[1] | Section 10 Permits | | Section 404 Permits | | Section 10 & 404 Permits | | All Permits | |
|---|---|---|---|---|---|---|---|---|
| | # | % | # | % | # | % | # | % |
| A | 416 | 12 | 107 | 24 | 302 | 11 | 825 | 13 |
| B | 20 | * | 7 | 2 | 28 | 1 | 55 | * |
| C | 2,904 | 87 | 333 | 74 | 2,316 | 88 | 5,553 | 86 |
| D | 49 | 32 | 20 | 20 | 25 | 18 | 94 | 24 |
| E | 78 | 51 | 67 | 66 | 75 | 55 | 220 | 56 |
| F | 25 | 16 | 14 | 14 | 37 | 27 | 76 | 19 |
| G | 152 | 100 | 101 | 100 | 137 | 100 | 390 | 100 |

Table 30e.  DREDGE & FILL PERMITS (A TO C) AND REPORTED VIOLATIONS (D TO G) --
Districts Los Angelos, California through Seattle, Washington

| Action[1] | Section 10 Permits | | Section 404 Permits | | Section 10 & 404 Permits | | All Permits | |
|---|---|---|---|---|---|---|---|---|
| | # | % | # | % | # | % | # | % |
| A | 178 | 19 | 63 | 40 | 103 | 24 | 344 | 23 |
| B | 5 | * | 1 | * | 9 | 2 | 15 | * |
| C | 749 | 80 | 95 | 60 | 319 | 74 | 1,163 | 76 |
| D | 77 | 22 | 11 | 10 | 19 | 20 | 107 | 19 |
| E | 264 | 75 | 90 | 82 | 67 | 71 | 421 | 76 |
| F | 10 | 3 | 9 | 8 | 9 | 9 | 28 | 5 |
| G | 351 | 100 | 110 | 100 | 95 | 100 | 556 | 100 |

_____

| [1] | | Action | Meaning |
|---|---|---|---|
| Application | | A | Cancelled or withdrawn |
| " | | B | Denied |
| " | | C | Permit or Letter of Permission issued |
| Violations | | D | After the fact applications accepted |
| " | | E | Permit not necessary, or reported violation already under permit |
| " | | F | Submitted for litigation |
| " | | G | Sum of D, E and F |

* Less than 1%
Source:  U.S. Army Corps of Engineers data.

SOME DREDGE AND FILL PERMITS ALLOW DREDGING OF VALUABLE WETLANDS.
This photograph is from Davis, North Carolina (Conservation Foundation
photo by M. Fahay).

# 31. WETLAND ANIMALS

The 1954 wetlands survey of the U.S. Fish and Wildlife Service listed 25 species of game and fur animals which make use of coastal wetlands. The report also discussed more generally the use of wetlands by migratory birds. These species were discussed because they are widely known or used directly by man. Numerous other animals, both terrestial and aquatic, are found in wetlands, or depend in some way on wetlands. Some of these are listed in Table 39. The wetland types are described in Table 27.

Table 31a.   USE OF WETLAND TYPES BY GAME AND FUR ANIMALS.

| Species: | Number of States Reporting Use in Wetland Type | | | | | | | | |
|---|---|---|---|---|---|---|---|---|---|
| | 12 | 13 | 14 | 15 | 16 | 17 | 18 | 19 | 20 |
| Small Game: | | | | | | | | | |
| Gallinules | 7 | 7 | 6 | 1 | 1 | 1 | 1 | -- | -- |
| Grouse, Sage | 1 | 1 | -- | -- | 1 | -- | 1 | 1 | -- |
| Mourning dove | 1 | 1 | -- | 2 | -- | -- | -- | -- | -- |
| Pheasant | 7 | 2 | -- | -- | 2 | -- | 1 | -- | -- |
| Quail, Bobwhite | 4 | -- | -- | -- | 1 | -- | -- | -- | -- |
| Rails | 12 | 11 | 4 | 5 | 9 | 8 | 10 | -- | 1 |
| Rabbit, Cottontail | 9 | 2 | -- | -- | -- | -- | -- | -- | -- |
| Rabbit, Swamp | 4 | 3 | -- | 1 | 4 | 3 | 3 | -- | -- |
| Snipe | 10 | 5 | -- | 3 | 4 | 3 | 4 | 3 | -- |
| Woodcock | 5 | 1 | -- | -- | -- | -- | -- | -- | -- |
| Big Game: | | | | | | | | | |
| White-tailed deer | 6 | 5 | -- | 1 | 1 | 1 | 2 | -- | -- |
| Black-tailed deer | 1 | 1 | -- | 1 | 2 | -- | 2 | 2 | -- |
| Fur Animals: | | | | | | | | | |
| Beaver | 4 | 4 | 1 | -- | 1 | -- | 2 | 1 | -- |
| Bobcat | 1 | 1 | -- | -- | -- | -- | -- | -- | -- |
| Fox (Red and Gray) | 10 | 5 | -- | 1 | 8 | 2 | 7 | 1 | -- |
| Mink | 16 | 13 | 9 | -- | 4 | 4 | 7 | 3 | -- |
| Muskrat | 16 | 16 | 11 | 1 | 10 | 5 | 11 | 3 | -- |
| Nutria | 1 | 1 | 1 | -- | -- | 1 | -- | -- | -- |
| Opossum | 4 | -- | -- | -- | -- | 1 | -- | -- | -- |
| Otter | 13 | 12 | 10 | -- | 5 | -- | 5 | 1 | -- |
| Raccoon | 17 | 12 | 11 | 2 | 11 | 6 | 10 | 5 | -- |
| Skunk | 4 | 4 | 1 | 1 | 1 | 1 | 1 | 1 | -- |
| Weasel | 2 | 2 | -- | -- | -- | -- | -- | -- | -- |
| Alligator | 3 | 3 | 1 | -- | 1 | 1 | -- | -- | -- |

Table 31b.  NUMBER OF GAME AND FUR SPECIES USING WETLANDS BY STATE.

| State | Number of Species Using Wetland Type | | | | | | | | |
|-------|-----|-----|-----|-----|-----|-----|-----|-----|-----|
|       | 12  | 13  | 14  | 15  | 16  | 17  | 18  | 19  | 20  |
| Alabama        | 5  | 2  | -- | -- | -- | 6  | -- | -- | -- |
| California     | 4  | 4  | 4  | -- | -- | -- | 1  | 1  | -- |
| Connecticut    | 8  | 6  | 5  | -- | 5  | -- | 4  | -- | -- |
| Delaware       | 9  | 4  | 3  | -- | 4  | -- | 4  | -- | -- |
| Florida        | 7  | 6  | 1  | 1  | -- | 4  | 4  | -- | 1  |
| Georgia        | 12 | 3  | 3  | 2  | 4  | 5  | 5  | -- | -- |
| Louisiana      | 19 | 19 | 4  | 4  | 6  | 5  | 3  | -- | -- |
| Maine          | 5  | 4  | 4  | -- | 3  | -- | 3  | 3  | -- |
| Maryland       | 4  | 2  | 2  | -- | 2  | 2  | 2  | 2  | -- |
| Massachusetts  | 10 | 9  | 4  | -- | 3  | -- | 3  | -- | -- |
| Mississippi    | 11 | 7  | 5  | 4  | 6  | 6  | 5  | 1  | -- |
| New Hampshire  | 9  | 6  | 4  | -- | 8  | -- | 6  | 5  | -- |
| New Jersey     | 9  | 7  | 4  | -- | 7  | -- | 7  | 5  | -- |
| New York       | 8  | 6  | 5  | -- | 7  | -- | 6  | 1  | -- |
| North Carolina | 5  | 2  | 1  | -- | -- | 4  | 2  | -- | -- |
| Oregon         | 6  | 6  | -- | -- | 6  | -- | 6  | 6  | -- |
| Rhode Island   | 8  | 6  | 4  | -- | -- | -- | -- | -- | -- |
| South Carolina | 7  | 4  | 3  | 1  | 2  | 3  | 3  | -- | -- |
| Texas          | 4  | 4  | -- | -- | -- | -- | -- | -- | -- |
| Virginia       | 12 | 10 | 4  | 5  | 5  | 3  | 3  | -- | -- |
| Washington     | -- | -- | -- | 2  | 2  | -- | 5  | 3  | -- |

Source:  U.S. Department of the Interior, Fish and Wildlife Service. Wetlands of the United States: Their extent and their value to waterfowl and other wildlife.  Circular 39.

# VII  LIVING RESOURCES

In 1880 the fisheries of the United States and Alaska brought in 1.7 billion pounds of fish whose value was 39 million dollars.  By 1979, the weight of the catch had increased by 3.7 times, and the value of the catch had increaed by 57 times.  The 6 billion dollar a year commercial fishery provides high quality protein to eat, and oils for a variety of commercial uses.

The recreational fishery provides additional fishes for food and also for recreation.  In 1970, the recreational catch was 24% of the total catch.  The fisheries are a resource which is susceptible to human interference whether it be overfishing, pollution, or placing dams in the path of fish migrating upstream to spawn such as the shad and salmon.

Other species live in the coast too.  Table 39 provides an example of a species which is making a comeback from near extinction, while Table 40 lists species which are presently close to extinction.

# 32. FISHERIES HISTORY

The retail value of the domestic fisheries landings in 1979 was over six billion dollars. This catch is heavily derived from nearshore waters. The catch of six species (Table 32b) has historically accounted for about half the value of the fishery. These species are either entirely, or partially (usually for the purpose of reproduction, or as a nursery for juveniles) estuarine dwelling, although only some species of shrimp are ever estuarine dwelling. For the fishery as a whole, about half of the catch (by value) is caught within 3 miles of shore. The percentage caught within 3 miles of shore by weight is even greater. In 1975, for example, 60% of the weight of the catch came from within 3 miles of shore. (Source same as table)

Annual domestic fishery landings from 1950 to 1977 have weighed about 5 billion pounds. In 1978, the catch reached 6 billion pounds. Whether the 1978 and 1979 catches are a product of the recently initiated 200-mile Fishery Conservation zone (The Fishery Conservation and Management Act) is unknown. However, recent increases are in species not managed under the FCMA. The dockside value of the catch has grown from 99 million dollars in 1940 to over 1800 million in 1978. Commercial fisheries have historically provided employment to over 200,000 people. The recent year of greatest income for fishermen (adjusted for inflation) was 1973. A GNP deflator was used to adjust for inflation.

Table 32a.   HISTORY OF DOMESTIC FISHERY LANDINGS.

| Year | Retail Value (in millions of dollars) | Dockside Value (in millions of dollars) | Catch Weight (in billions of pounds) | Percentage of Catch Caught within 3 miles of shore (by dockside value) |
|---|---|---|---|---|
| 1979 | 6,352 | 2,234 | 6.3 | 49 |
| 1978 | 5,994 | 1,854 | 6.0 | 4G |
| 1977 | 5,437 | 1,515 | 5.2 | 49 |
| 1976 | 3,754 | 1,353 | 5.3 | 47 |
| 1975 | 3,008 | 971 | 4.8 | 47 |
| 1974 | 3,004 | 899 | 4.9 | 51 |
| 1973 | 2,801 | 907 | 4.7 | 49 |
| 1972 | 2,129 | 704 | 4.7 | 41 |
| 1971 | 1,968 | 643 | 5.0 | 46 |
| 1970 | 1,850 | 613 | 4.9 | -- |
| 1960 | -- | 354 | 4.9 | -- |
| 1950 | -- | 347 | 4.9 | -- |
| 1940 | -- | 99 | 4.1 | -- |
| 1930[1] | -- | 104 | 3.3 | -- |
| 1920 | -- | 78 | 2.2 | -- |
| 1908 | -- | 51 | 1.8 | -- |
| 1900 | -- | 43 | 1.8 | -- |
| 1880 | -- | 39 | 1.6 | -- |

[1] catch of 1920 and earlier refer to U.S. catch without Alaska.
Source:   1930-1880: U.S. Department of Commerce, U.S. Bureau of the Census, 1960. Historical Statistics of the United States Colonial Times to 1957.

THE <u>HOLLY F. MURPHY</u> AND <u>CAPTAIN STACY II</u>, two trawlers, berthed at
Morehead City, California.   The booms on each boat hold the trawls open.
(photo by Mark Hooper)

Table 32b. HISTORY OF COMMERCIAL LANDINGS OF SELECTED SPECIES (IN MILLIONS OF DOLLARS).

| Year | Menhaden | Shrimp | Salmon | Blue Crabs | Oysters | Clams | Total |
|------|----------|--------|--------|------------|---------|-------|-------|
| 1979 | 109 | 472 | 413 | 31 | 66 | 79 | 1170 |
| 1978 | 98 | 386 | 255 | 28 | 61 | 74 | 902 |
| 1977 | 68 | 355 | 221 | 27 | 53 | 74 | 798 |
| 1976 | 67 | 331 | 196 | 23 | 53 | 63 | 733 |
| 1975 | 49 | 226 | 116 | 19 | 43 | 41 | 494 |
| 1974 | 66 | 178 | 121 | 19 | 34 | 39 | 457 |
| 1973 | 73 | 219 | 125 | 17 | 35 | 35 | 504 |
| 1972 | 31 | 193 | 63 | 14 | 34 | 32 | 367 |
| 1971 | 36 | 167 | 78 | 12 | 30 | 31 | 354 |
| 1970 | 34 | 130 | 99 | 10 | 29 | 29 | 331 |

Table 32c. HISTORY OF FISHERIES EMPLOYMENT.

| Year | Number Employed as Fishermen | Number Employed in Processing and Wholesaling | Total |
|------|------------------------------|-----------------------------------------------|-------|
| 1975 | 168,013 | 92,310 | 260,323 |
| 1970 | 140,538 | 86,813 | 227,351 |
| 1965 | 128,565 | 86,864 | 215,429 |
| 1960 | 130,431 | 93,625 | 224,056 |
| 1950 | 161,463 | 102,015 | 263,478 |
| 1940 | 124,795 | 90,215 | 215,010 |
| 1930 | 119,716 | 78,996 | 198,712 |

Table 32d. VALUE OF THE CATCH IN CONSTANT DOLLARS PER FISHERMAN.

| Year | No. Fisherman | Dockside Value (in millions of dollars) | Constant Dollar Value (in millions of 1972 dollars) | Dockside Value Per Fisherman | Constant Dollar Value Per Fisherman |
|------|---------------|------------------------------------------|------------------------------------------------------|------------------------------|-------------------------------------|
| 1975 | 168,000 | 971 | 763 | 5,780 | 4,543 |
| 1974 | 161,000 | 899 | 775 | 5,584 | 4,814 |
| 1973 | 149,000 | 907 | 857 | 6,087 | 5,754 |
| 1972 | 139,000 | 704 | 704 | 5,065 | 5,065 |
| 1970 | 141,000 | 613 | 671 | 4,347 | 4,757 |
| 1965 | 129,000 | 446 | 600 | 3,457 | 4,653 |
| 1960 | 130,000 | 354 | 515 | 2,723 | 3,964 |
| 1955 | 144,000 | 347 | 568 | 2,410 | 3,950 |
| 1950 | 161,000 | 99 | 185 | 615 | 1,147 |

Source: U.S. Department of Commerce, NOAA, NMFS. 1973. Fishery Statistics of the United States 1970. NMFS Statistical Digest No. 64; Fisheries of the United States, Annual Reports for the Years 1979 to 1971. NMFS Current Fisheries Statistics 8000, 7800, 7500, 7200, 6900, 6700, 6400, 6100, 5900; U.S. Department of Commerce; U.S. Bureau of the Census, 1979. Statistical Abstract of the United States: 1979.

# 33. RECORD CATCHES

In recent decades the value of the catch has increased, but the weight of the catch has remained fairly constant. However, the peak weight of the catch is long past in many states. Only five states have recorded peak catches in the 1970's (Virginia, Alabama, Mississippi, Louisiana and Oregon), while 3 states (Rhode Island, New York, Maryland) recorded their peak catches in the last century.

Table 33. CURRENT CATCH COMPARED TO RECORD CATCH BY STATE.

| State | Year of Record Catch (Pounds) | $\dfrac{\text{1978 Catch}}{\text{Record Catch}}$ x 100% |
|---|---|---|
| Maine | 1950 | 53.4 |
| New Hampshire | -- | -- |
| Massachusetts | 1948 | 58.0 |
| Rhode Island | 1899 | 65.4 |
| Connecticut | 1930 | 5.7 |
| New York | 1880 | 10.8 |
| New Jersey | 1956 | 30.3 |
| Delaware | 1953 | 0.3 |
| Maryland | 1890 | 42.2 |
| Virginia | 1972 | 80.9 |
| North Carolina | 1959 | 87.4 |
| South Carolina | 1965 | 77.4 |
| Georgia | 1927 | 36.7 |
| Florida | 1938 | 71.0 |
| Alabama | 1973 | 79.4 |
| Mississippi | 1971 | 94.2 |
| Louisiana | 1978 | 100.0 |
| Texas | 1960 | 43.6 |
| California | 1936 | 41.0 |
| Oregon | 1978 | 100.0 |
| Washington | 1941 | 70.1 |

Source: U.S. Department of Commerce, NOAA, NMFS. 1979. Fisheries of the United States, 1978. NMFS, Current Fisheries Statistics, No. 7800.

# 34. STATE FISHERIES

Six billion pounds of fish were landed at a dockside value of 1.8 billion dollars in 1978. Louisiana, California, and Virginia landed almost half of the total catch. California, Louisiana, and Massachusetts were the three leading states by value of the catch in 1978; their combined catch was over thirty percent of the total value of the catch. (Both rankings are exclusive of Alaska which would be second by weight of catch, and first in the value of the catch.)

Table 34.  STATE LANDINGS -- 1978.

| | Thousands of Pounds | Percent | Rank | Thousands of Dollars | Percent | Rank |
|---|---|---|---|---|---|---|
| Maine | 190,203 | 3.7 | 7 | 68,833 | 5.0 | 7 |
| New Hampshire | 4,862 | 0.09 | 21 | 1,750 | 0.1 | 20 |
| Massachusetts | 376,878 | 7.3 | 5 | 152,251 | 11.0 | 3 |
| Rhode Island | 83,721 | 1.6 | 13 | 29,308 | 2.1 | 15 |
| Connecticut | 5,053 | 0.1 | 19 | 4,368 | 0.3 | 19 |
| New York | 36,340 | 0.7 | 15 | 33,870 | 2.4 | 13 |
| New Jersey | 163,685 | 3.2 | 9 | 44,432 | 3.2 | 10 |
| Delaware | 1,056 | 0.02 | 20 | 500 | 0.04 | 21 |
| Maryland | 59,726 | 1.2 | 14 | 33,557 | 2.4 | 14 |
| Virginia | 538,892 | 10.5 | 3 | 60,622 | 4.4 | 8 |
| North Carolina | 299,536 | 5.8 | 6 | 40,607 | 2.9 | 11 |
| South Carolina | 20,610 | 0.4 | 17 | 16,031 | 1.2 | 17 |
| Georgia | 17,493 | 0.3 | 18 | 14,597 | 1.1 | 18 |
| Florida | 171,462 | 3.3 | 8 | 97,519 | 7.0 | 5 |
| Alabama | 31,553 | 0.6 | 16 | 35,922 | 2.6 | 12 |
| Mississippi | 377,534 | 7.3 | 4 | 28,291 | 2.0 | 16 |
| Louisiana | 1,673,922 | 32.5 | 1 | 190,167 | 13.7 | 2 |
| Texas | 103,524 | 2.0 | 12 | 148,901 | 10.8 | 4 |
| California | 722,311 | 14.0 | 2 | 228,238 | 16.5 | 1 |
| Oregon | 134,657 | 2.6 | 11 | 56,600 | 4.1 | 9 |
| Washington | 138,301 | 2.7 | 10 | 97,178 | 7.0 | 6 |
| TOTAL (Excluding Alaska & Hawaii Excluding non-coastal) | 5,151,319 | 85.5 | | 1,383,542 | 74.6 | |
| Alaska | 745,586 | 12.4 | | 438,616 | 23.6 | |
| Hawaii | 14,575 | 0.2 | | 11,620 | 0.6 | |
| Non coastal | 116,220 | 1.9 | | 20,752 | 1.1 | |
| TOTAL | 6,027,799 | | | 1,854,530 | | |

Source:  U.S. Department of Commerce, NOAA, MNFS. 1979.  Fisheries of the United States, 1978.  Current Fisheries Statistics No. 7800.

# 35. FISHERIES PORTS

San Pedro, California was the leading fisheries port in the nation both by value and weight of the catch from 1976 through 1978 (3 year average). San Pedro achieves this status because it is the port of record for much of the fish caught in the Pacific Ocean. New Bedford, and Gloucester are the leading North Atlantic ports; Key West and Beaufort-Morehead City are the leading South Atlantic ports. Among Gulf Coast ports Brownsville-Port Isabel, Texas and Cameron, Louisiana lead (these ports are listed by value and weight, respectively.) While there are many ports in the country, the top twenty account for about half of the weight and value of the catch. We have combined three years worth of data rather than present just the most recent data to smooth out temporary increases and decreases of ports.

Table 35a.  TOP 20 U.S. FISHERIES PORTS -- 1976-1978 BY VALUE OF CATCH.

| Port | Millions of Dollars (3 year average) | Percentage of Total U.S. Catch Value | Cumulative Percent |
|------|------|------|------|
| San Pedro, CA | 106.1 | 6.7 | 6.7 |
| Dutch Harbor, AK | 69.8 | 4.4 | 11.1 |
| Kodiak, AK | 67.7 | 4.3 | 15.4 |
| San Diego, CA | 47.7 | 3.0 | 18.5 |
| New Bedford, MA | 45.6 | 2.9 | 21.4 |
| Brownsville-Port Isabel, TX | 39.3 | 2.5 | 23.9 |
| Dulac-Chavin, LA | 37.5 | 2.3 | 26.2 |
| Aransas Pass-Rockport, TX | 35.3 | 2.2 | 28.5 |
| Freeport, TX | 25.6 | 1.6 | 30.1 |
| Ketchikan, AK | 25.1 | 1.6 | 31.7 |
| Cameron, LA | 24.9 | 1.5 | 33.3 |
| Bayou La Batre, AL | 24.1 | 1.5 | 34.8 |
| Gloucester, MA | 22.3 | 1.4 | 36.3 |
| Empire-Venice, LA | 20.3 | 1.2 | 37.5 |
| Cape May-Wildwood, NJ | 20.1 | 1.2 | 38.8 |
| Petersburg, AK | 18.7 | 1.1 | 40.0 |
| Akutan, AK | 18.5 | 1.1 | 41.2 |
| Key West, FL | 18.3 | 1.1 | 42.4 |
| Golden Meadow-Leeville, LA | 17.8 | 1.1 | 45.5 |
| Eureka, CA | 16.6 | 1.0 | 44.5 |

TABLE 35b.  TOP 20 U.S. FISHERIES PORTS -- 1976-1978 BY WEIGHT OF CATCH.

| Port | Millions of Pounds (3 year average) | Percentage of Total U.S. Catch Weight | Cumulative Percent |
|---|---|---|---|
| San Pedro, CA | 494.4 | 8.9 | 8.9 |
| Cameron, LA | 432.7 | 7.8 | 16.7 |
| Pascagoula-Moss Pt., MS | 275.2 | 4.9 | 21.7 |
| Empire-Venice, LA | 232.4 | 4.2 | 25.9 |
| Dulac-Chauvin, LA | 230.3 | 4.1 | 30.1 |
| Kodiak, AK | 169.5 | 3.0 | 33.2 |
| Gloucester, MA | 160.1 | 2.9 | 36.1 |
| San Diego, CA | 131.0 | 2.3 | 38.4 |
| Dutch Harbor, AK | 105.8 | 1.9 | 40.3 |
| Beaufort-Morehead City, NC | 96.1 | 1.7 | 42.1 |
| New Bedford, MA | 70.7 | 1.2 | 43.4 |
| Pt. Judith, RI | 55.3[2] | 1.0 | 44.4 |
| Ketchikan, AK | 55.2[1] | 1.0 | 45.4 |
| Biloxi, MS | 47.6 | 0.8 | 46.2 |
| Cape May-Wildwood, NJ | 45.1 | 0.8 | 47.0 |
| Eureka, CA | 42.8 | 0.7 | 47.8 |
| Rockland, ME | 40.1[2] | 0.7 | 48.5 |
| Bellingham, WA | 35.5[1] | 0.6 | 49.2 |
| Portland, ME | 34.5 | 0.6 | 49.8 |
| Astoria, OR | 34.2 | 0.6 | 50.4 |

[1] Based on 1977 and 1978
[2] Based on 1978

Source:  U.S. Department of Commerce, NOAA, NMFS.  Fisheries of the United States, Annual Reports for the Years 1978 through 1976.  NMFS Current Fisheries Statistics 7800, 7500, 7200.

# 36. COMMERCIAL FISHERIES

Not only does the commercial fisheries catch vary between states, but so does the catch per fisherman. New York has the lowest weight of catch per fisherman, while Mississippi has the highest weight of catch per fisherman; 39 times that of a New York fisherman. The range in value of catch per fisherman is also broad. A Texas fisherman lands a catch worth 6.8 times that of a Maryland fisherman.

In order to determine catch per fisherman, we combined full and part-time fisherman by counting each part-time fisherman as one-half of a full-time fisherman. A full-time fisherman is defined as someone who receives more than half his annual income from fishing. Part-time fisherman receive less than half their annual income from fishing. It was not possible to make this distinction for California, or most other Pacific fishermen.

Table 36. COMMERCIAL CATCH PER FISHERMAN -- 1974.

| | Full Time | Part Time | Weight of Catch (Thousands of Pounds) | Value of Catch (Thousands) of Dollars) | Thousands of Pounds Per Fisherman | Thousands of Dollars Per Fisherman |
|---|---|---|---|---|---|---|
| Maine | 6,863 | 11,330 | 138,352 | 48,499 | 11.04 | 3.87 |
| New Hampshire | 98 | 406 | 3,146 | 1,277 | 10.45 | 4.24 |
| Massachusetts | 4,420 | 4,812 | 273,753 | 82,873 | 40.10 | 12.14 |
| Rhode Island | 1,505 | 1,687 | 79,483 | 18,899 | 33.84 | 8.05 |
| Connecticut | 392 | 722 | 3,629 | 2,584 | 4.82 | 3.43 |
| New York | 3,176 | 9,385 | 37,422 | 28,263 | 4.76 | 3.59 |
| New Jersey | 1,947 | 1,134 | 143,582 | 19,812 | 57.11 | 7.88 |
| Delaware | 205 | 349 | 7,055 | 1,717 | 18.59 | 4.52 |
| Maryland | 4,459 | 11,774 | 64,317 | 22,898 | 6.22 | 2.21 |
| Virginia | 4,556 | 3,530 | 444,827 | 33,076 | 70.37 | 5.23 |
| North Carolina | 2,832 | 1,908 | 238,301 | 20,000 | 62.94 | 5.28 |
| South Carolina | 1,304 | 467 | 20,079 | 13,117 | 13.06 | 8.53 |
| Georgia | 1,304 | 459 | 17,750 | 11,947 | 11.57 | 7.79 |
| Florida (Atlantic) | 2,168 | 642 | 56,943 | 18,512 | 22.88 | 7.44 |
| Florida (Gulf) | 6,699 | 1,793 | 115,836 | 56,531 | 15.25 | 7.44 |
| Alabama | 1,615 | 180 | 31,564 | 21,016 | 18.51 | 12.33 |
| Mississippi | 1,442 | 406 | 305,758 | 14,347 | 185.87 | 8.72 |
| Louisiana | 9,101 | 2,247 | 1,114,898 | 86,028 | 109.04 | 8.41 |
| Texas | 5,945 | 520 | 85,980 | 92,659 | 13.86 | 14.93 |
| California | 16,681 | --- | 874,978 | 134,737 | 52.45 | 8.08 |
| Oregon | 4,486 | 18 | 86,229 | 26,015 | 19.18 | 5.79 |
| Washington | 10,505 | 339 | 146,021 | 61,581 | 13.68 | 5.77 |
| TOTAL | 91,703 | 54,108 | | | | |

Source: Adapted from U.S. Department of Commerce, NOAA, NMFS. Fisheries Statistics of the United States 1974. Statistical Digest No. 6700.

# 37. RECREATIONAL FISHERIES

Many people participate in the recreational fishery, and much of their catch is at some point in its life cycle estuarine dwelling. These tables give characteristics of the recreational catch for selected estuarine species. Sea trout were landed in largest numbers of any of these species in 1960, 1965, and again in 1970. Croaker, and flatfishes also comprise a large proportion of estuarine species landed. The data were collected by the National Oceanic and Atmospheric Administration (NOAA, a part of the Department of Commerce). No study was made of the 1975 fishery, but studies are forthcoming for the 1979 and 1980 fisheries. An individual is counted as an angler for each species that he or she catches. For this reason, addition of the total number of anglers is not a meaningful statistic.

The data for participants in the recreational fishery is given under the Recreational heading (Section 9).

Table 37a. ESTUARINE RECREATIONAL FISHERIES -- NUMBER OF FISH BY YEAR.

|  | 1970 | 1965 | 1960 |
|---|---|---|---|
|  |  | (THOUSANDS OF FISH) |  |
| Bluefish | 36,458 | 30,525 | 23,814 |
| Catfish | 56,265 | 41,739 | 32,695 |
| Croaker | 66,016 | 51,134 | 45,577 |
| Black Drum | 14,710 | 5,676 | 9,577 |
| Red Drum | 18,164 | 11,195 | 15,277 |
| American Eel | 3,111 | 4,118 | 2,079 |
| Flatfish* | 52,078 | 48,432 | 44,895 |
| Mullet | 4,283 | 18,448 | 19,240 |
| Chinook Salmon | 912 | 856 | 468 |
| Coho Salmon | 1,447 | 1,384 | 364 |
| Sea Trout | 96,825 | 87,615 | 83,836 |
| Striped Bass | 16,268 | 18,251 | 12,402 |
| Steelhead | 724 | 427 | 675 |
| TOTAL | 367,261 | 319,800 | 290,899 |

Table 37b.   ESTUARINE RECREATIONAL FISHERIES -- NUMBER OF ANGLERS BY YEAR

|  | 1970 | 1965 | 1960 |
|---|---|---|---|
|  | (THOUSANDS OF ANGLERS) | | |
| Bluefish | 1,440 | 955 | 899 |
| Catfish | 1,300 | 679 | 803 |
| Croaker | 1,372 | 1,200 | 933 |
| Black Drum | 478 | 318 | 465 |
| Red Drum | 864 | 777 | 639 |
| American Eel | 363 | 326 | 159 |
| Flatfish* | 2,548 | 2,168 | 1,967 |
| Mullet | 71 | 258 | 92 |
| Chinook Salmon | 218 | 186 | 126 |
| Coho Salmon | 321 | 305 | 133 |
| Sea Trout | 1,806 | 1,415 | 1,269 |
| Striped Bass | 946 | 866 | 687 |
| Steel Head | 116 | 38 | 66 |

Table 37c.   ESTUARINE RECREATIONAL FISHERIES -- WEIGHT OF FISH CAUGHT BY YEAR.

|  | 1970 | 1965 | 1960 |
|---|---|---|---|
|  | (POUNDS OF FISH) | | |
| Bluefish | 120,811 | 93,209 | 50,680 |
| Catfish | 72,510 | 50,598 | 36,980 |
| Croaker | 75,436 | 39,292 | 31,340 |
| Black Drum | 42,677 | 38,357 | 42,630 |
| Red Drum | 66,486 | 44,740 | 71,500 |
| American Eel | 4,123 | 4,073 | 2,170 |
| Flatfish* | 76,883 | 77,416 | 59,320 |
| Mullet | 2,281 | 22,100 | 17,480 |
| Chinook Salmon | 15,171 | 11,276 | 5,800 |
| Coho Salmon | 14,356 | 12,167 | 2,690 |
| Sea Trout | 136,888 | 135,413 | 130,680 |
| Striped Bass | 83,783 | 70,991 | 57,260 |
| Steelhead | 4,441 | 1,614 | 4,590 |
| TOTAL | 715,846 | 601,246 | 513,120 |

37d.  ESTUARINE RECREATIONAL FISHERIES -- NUMBER OF FISH PER ANGLER.

|                | 1970 | 1965 | 1960  |
|----------------|------|------|-------|
| Bluefish       | 25.3 | 32.0 | 26.5  |
| Catfish        | 43.3 | 61.5 | 40.7  |
| Croaker        | 48.1 | 42.6 | 48.8  |
| Black Drum     | 30.8 | 17.8 | 20.6  |
| Red Drum       | 21.0 | 14.4 | 23.9  |
| American Eel   | 8.6  | 12.6 | 13.1  |
| Flatfish*      | 20.4 | 22.3 | 22.8  |
| Mullet         | 60.3 | 71.5 | 209.1 |
| Chinook Salmon | 4.2  | 4.6  | 3.7   |
| Coho Salmon    | 4.5  | 4.5  | 2.7   |
| Sea Trout      | 53.6 | 61.9 | 66.1  |
| Striped Bass   | 17.2 | 21.1 | 18.1  |
| Steelhead      | 6.2  | 11.2 | 10.2  |

---

\*  The flatfish category includes winter and summer flounder, but excludes Pacific flatfishes.

Source:  Adapted from  U.S. Department of Commerce, NOAA, NMFS.  The 1970 Saltwater Angling Survey.  Current Fisheries Statistics 6200; U.S. Department of the Interior, Bureau of Sport Fisheries and Wildlife.  1968.  The 1965 Salt-water Angling Survey.  Resource Publication 67;  U.S. Department of the Interior, Bureau of Sport Fisheries and Wildlife.  The 1960 Salt-Water Angling Survey. Circular 153.

# 38. RECREATIONAL FISHERIES

The 1970 recreational catch yielded 1.58 billion pounds of fishes. The commercial catch for 1970 was 4.9 billion pounds. Thus, recreational fisheries accounted for 24% of the total catch in 1970. The highest proportion of the recreational catch was landed in the South Atlantic Region. Within any given region, about 15 species or species groups will account for 95% of the fish caught (the 1970 survey lists 79 species or species groups in all). In a given region the most common fish landed typically accounts for 20% of the catch. In total, the Spotted Seatrout, the Croaker, and Catfishes were the three most commonly caught species.

Table 38.  LEADING SPECIES IN THE 1970 RECREATIONAL FISH CATCH (BY NUMBER OF FISH CAUGHT) BY REGION.

| Maine through New York | % | Cumulative % | New Jersey to Cape Hatteras, North Carolina | % | Cumulative % |
|---|---|---|---|---|---|
| Atlantic Mackerels | 29 | 29 | Spot | 20 | 20 |
| Winter Flounders | 18 | 47 | Puffers | 16 | 36 |
| Puffers | 9 | 57 | Atlantic Mackerels | 11 | 47 |
| Bluefish | 9 | 66 | Perches | 9 | 56 |
| Summer Flounders | 7 | 73 | Bluefish | 7 | 63 |
| Striped bass | 4 | 77 | Striped Bass | 6 | 69 |
| Tautog | 4 | 80 | Weakfish | 6 | 75 |
| Cods | 3 | 83 | Winter Flounders | 4 | 79 |
| Porgies | 2 | 86 | Searobins | 4 | 83 |
| Searobins | 2 | 88 | Croakers | 3 | 85 |
| Kingfishes | 2 | 91 | Summer Flounders | 2 | 88 |
| Conner | 2 | 93 | Black sea basses | 2 | 90 |
| American Eel | 2 | 95 | Yellow Perch | 2 | 92 |
| TOTAL Number Caught | 117,014,000 | | Miscellaneous | 2 | 94 |
| TOTAL Pounds Caught | 267,451,000 | | Catfishes | 1 | 95 |
| | (17% of Total) | | TOTAL Number Caught | 168,209,000 | |
| | | | TOTAL Weight Caught | 246,267,000 | |
| | | | | (16% of Total) | |

Table 38.  LEADING SPECIES IN THE 1970 RECREATIONAL FISH CATCH (BY NUMBER
OF FISH CAUGHT) BY REGION (cont.).

### Cape Hatteras, North Carolina through Florida Keys

| | % | Cumulative % |
|---|---|---|
| Grunts | 12 | 12 |
| Porgies | 9 | 21 |
| Kingfishes | 8 | 29 |
| Spotted Seatrout | 8 | 36 |
| Bluefish | 7 | 43 |
| Spot | 7 | 50 |
| Catfishes | 6 | 56 |
| Yellowtail Snapper | 6 | 62 |
| Puffers | 5 | 67 |
| Croakers | 5 | 72 |
| Jacks | 4 | 75 |
| Black Seabasses | 4 | 79 |
| Black Drum | 3 | 82 |
| Spanish Mackerels | 3 | 85 |
| Red Drum | 3 | 88 |
| Groupers | 2 | 90 |
| King Mackerel | 2 | 92 |
| Summer Flounders | 2 | 94 |
| Snook | 1 | 95 |
| TOTAL Number Caught | 184,177,000 | |
| TOTAL Pounds Caught | 403,913,000 (26% of Total) | |

### Florida Keys through Mississippi River Delta

| | % | Cumulative % |
|---|---|---|
| Croakers | 19 | 19 |
| Spotted Seatrout | 15 | 34 |
| Catfishes | 14 | 49 |
| Sand Seatrout | 12 | 60 |
| Porgies | 7 | 67 |
| Kingfishes | 6 | 74 |
| Grunts | 5 | 78 |
| Red Drum | 4 | 82 |
| Summer Flounders | 2 | 84 |
| Black Drum | 2 | 87 |
| Mullets | 2 | 89 |
| Red Snapper | 2 | 90 |
| Groupers | 2 | 92 |
| King Mackerel | 1 | 94 |
| Spanish Mackerels | 1 | 95 |
| TOTAL Number Caught | 188,888,000 | |
| TOTAL Pounds Caught | 334,120,000 | |
| | (21% of Total) | |

### Mississippi River Delta through Mexico

| | % | Cumulative % |
|---|---|---|
| Spotted Seatrout | 25 | 25 |
| Catfishes | 16 | 41 |
| Croakers | 14 | 55 |
| Grunts | 12 | 67 |
| Sand Seatrout | 8 | 75 |
| Red Drum | 6 | 81 |
| Black Drum | 5 | 87 |
| Kingfishes | 3 | 90 |
| Summer Flounders | 2 | 92 |
| Porgies | 2 | 94 |
| Snappers | 1 | 95 |
| TOTAL Number Caught | 97,708,000 | |
| TOTAL Pounds Caught | 151,608,000 | |
| | (10% of Total) | |

### Mexico through Pt. Concepcion, California

| | % | Cumulative |
|---|---|---|
| Pacific Basses | 19 | 19 |
| Surfperches | 18 | 37 |
| Bonitos | 11 | 48 |
| Rockfishes | 9 | 58 |
| California corbina | 8 | 65 |
| Croakers | 7 | 72 |
| California halibut | 7 | 79 |
| Barracudas | 5 | 83 |
| Miscellaneous | 3 | 86 |
| Sculpins and cabezon | 2 | 88 |
| Tunas | 2 | 91 |
| California yellowtail | 2 | 92 |
| Jack mackerel | 2 | 94 |
| Pacific flatfishes | 1 | 95 |
| TOTAL Number Caught | 37,221,000 | |
| TOTAL Weight Caught | 94,234,000 | |
| | (6% of Total) | |

Table 38.  LEADING SPECIES IN THE RECREATIONAL FISH CATCH (BY NUMBER
           OF FISH CAUGHT) BY REGION (cont.).

Pt. Concepcion through Alaska
    (excluding Canada)

|                       | %   | Cumulative % |
|-----------------------|-----|--------------|
| Smelts                | 18  | 18           |
| Rockfishes            | 12  | 30           |
| Pacific Flatfishes    | 9   | 39           |
| Striped Bass          | 8   | 47           |
| Sculpins and Cabezon  | 8   | 55           |
| Surfperches           | 7   | 62           |
| Miscellaneous         | 7   | 69           |
| Coho Salmon           | 6   | 75           |
| Cutthroat Trout       | 5   | 80           |
| Chinook Salmon        | 4   | 83           |
| Ling Cod              | 3   | 86           |
| Steelhead             | 3   | 89           |
| Cods                  | 2   | 92           |
| Sablefish             | 2   | 94           |
| Croakers              | 1   | 95           |
| TOTAL Number Caught   | 24,100,000       ||
| TOTAL Pounds Caught   | 79,230,000       ||
|                       | (5% of Total)    ||

Source:  Adapted from U.S. Department of Commerce, NOAA, NMFS.
         1970 Salt-Water Angling Survey.  Current Fisheries Statistics
         6200.

# 39. COLONIAL BIRDS

Herons were almost hunted to extinction early in this century for their feathers. They reestablished themselves, but are again in decline. This most recent decline may be due to loss of wetlands habitat (Source same as table). Herons live in colonies as do a number of other species. Associated with these colonies are a number of other species. (The birds belonging to each of these groups are given in the footnote to this table.)

The numbers of colonies listed here are a conservative count of coastal or near coastal colonies. They are thought to include all large colonies (more than 250 nests) and most medium colonies (50 to 250 nests). Many small colonies were found, but many were missed.

Of course, many other species of birds dwell in coastal habitats, or can otherwise be found at the coast. Many bird guides list coastal species, and the Audubon Society Christmas counts (published annually in the July issue of American Birds) census some bird populations at specific coastal locations.

Table 39. COASTAL COLONIES OF HERONS AND THEIR ALLIES.[1]

| State | Number of Coastal Colonies |
|---|---|
| Maine | 20 |
| New Hampshire | -- |
| Massachusetts | 14 |
| Rhode Island | 3 |
| Connecticut | 1 |
| New York | 21 |
| New Jersey | 18 |
| Delaware | 2 |
| Maryland | 29 |
| Virginia | 35 |
| North Carolina | 38 |
| South Carolina | 23 |
| Georgia | 28 |
| Florida (Atlantic Coast and Keys) | 73 |
| Alabama | 2 |
| Mississippi | 12 |
| Louisiana | 146 |
| Texas | 120 |

[1] Species of herons and allies included in census of Atlantic Coast Colonies.

Great blue heron**,*
Great white heron
Green heron
Little blue heron**,*
Cattle egret*,**
Reddish egret**,*
Great egret**,*
Snowy egret**,*
Louisiana heron*,**
Black-crowned night heron*,**
Yellow-crowned night heron*,**
Wood Stork
Glossy ibis**
White ibis*,**
Roseate Spoonbill**,*
White faced ibis*,**

Note: Only those species above the line are listed in the Atlantic Coast Census

* Listed in the Texas Colonial Waterbird Census.
** Listed in the Louisiana, Mississippi and Alabama survey.

Associated colonial and noncolonial species found breeding in Atlantic Coast heron colonies.

Brown pelican*,**
Double-crested cormorant
Anhinga*,**
Least bittern
Scarlet ibis[a]
Common eider
Bald eagle
Osprey
American oystercatcher**
Great black-backed gull
Herring gull
Laughing gull*,**
Gull-billed tern*,**
Forster's tern*,**
Common tern**
Least tern*,**
Royal tern*,**
Sandwich tern*,**
Black skimmer*,**
White Pelican*
Olivaceous cormorant*,**
Sooty tern*,**
Caspian tern*,**

[a] single record and not considered a regular nester.

[2] Only Mobile County.
Source: R.G. Osborn and T.W. Custer. 1978. Herons and Their Allies: Atlas of Atlantic Colonies, 1975 and 1976. U.S. Fish and Wildlife Service, Office of Biological Services. 211 pp.; Gene W. Blaclock et al. 1978. Texas Colonial Waterbird Census, 1973-1976. Texas Parks and Wildlife Department, FA Report Series No. 15; J.W. Portnoy. 1977. Nesting colonies of seabirds and wading birds--coastal Louisiana, Mississippi, and Alabama. U.S. Fish and Wildlife Service, Office of Biological Services. FWS/OBS-77/07. 126 pp.

COMMON EGRET in flight.  (Photo by Mark Hooper).

BABY HERONS in the nest.  (Photo by Irving Hooper).

# 40. ENDANGERED SPECIES

A species is the collection of populations of interbreeding, or potentially interbreeding organisms. Throughout time, species have evolved, and gone extinct for a great number of reasons. In some cases, man has accelerated this process of extinction by hunting, environmental contamination or other habitat alteration. The Endangered Species Act was passed in December 1973 in order to minimize man's extinction of species. Under the Act protection is afforded to plants, mammals, fishes, birds, amphibians, reptiles, and invertebrates (except for certain pest insects). It classifies species close to extinction as either endangered or threatened, and prescribes acts to promote their conservation. An endangered species is defined in the act as "any species [or subspecies] which is in danger of extinction throughout all or a significant part of its range." A threatened species is "any species [or subspecies] which is likely to become an endangered species within the forseeable future throughout all or a significant part of its range." The decision to place a species into one of these classifications rests primarily with the Department of Interior (although some species are under the jurisdiction of the Commerce Department) in consultation with the states, other federal agencies, and interested persons or organizations. These species are listed in the Federal Register.

The species given here are or were found in coastal counties. This list was provided by Dr. John Nagy and Mr. Charles E. Calef of the Brookhaven National Laboratory. He used a county list very similar to ours. The species in this table are only those actually listed (as opposed to proposed or candidate species) as of January 1, 1980.

The following notation is used in this table:

E  Endangered
T  Threatened
B  Either E or T depending on location
E* Extirpated from coastal counties.

ALLIGATORS ARE AN ENDANGERED SPECIES.  They lay one clutch of eggs per year which incubate for 90 days.  This 7.5 foot long mother alligator is opening her nest.  She has about 27 eggs inside and will carry roughly one-third of the hatchlings to the water in her mouth.  The rest will make it on their own.  Hunting has reduced alligators to their endangered status. (Okeefenokee National Wildlife Refuge in Georgia) (Photo by Eugene Meyers).

Table 40. ENDANGERED SPECIES.

| MAMMALS | ME | NH | MA | RI | CT | NY | NJ | DE | MD | VA | NC | SC | GA | FL | AL | MS | LA | TX | CA | OR | WA |
|---|---|---|---|---|---|---|---|---|---|---|---|---|---|---|---|---|---|---|---|---|---|
| 1) Myotis sodalis<br>   Bat, Indiana | | | | E | E | E | E | | E | | | | | | | | | | | | |
| 2) Ursus arctos horribilis<br>   Bear, Grizzly | | | | | | | | | | | | | | | | | | | T* | T* | T* |
| 3) Felis concolor couguar<br>   Cougar, Eastern | E* | | E* | E* | E* | E* | E* | E* | E* | E* | E* | E* | | | | | | | | | |
| 4) Odocoileus virginianus clavium<br>   Deer, Key | | | | | | | | | | | | | | E | | | | | | | |
| 5) Odocoileus virginianus leucurus<br>   Deer, White-tailed, Columbian | | | | | | | | | | | | | | | | | | | E | E | |
| 6) Vulpes macrotis mutica<br>   Fox, Kit, San Joaquin | | | | | | | | | | | | | | | | | | | E | | |
| 7) Panthera onca<br>   Jaguar | | | | | | | | | | | | | | | | | | E* | E* | | |
| 8) Felis yagouaroundi cacomitli<br>   Jaguarundi | | | | | | | | | | | | | | | | | | E | | | |
| 9) Trichechus manatus<br>   Manatee, West Indian (Florida) | | | | | | | | | | | E* | E* | E* | E* | E* | E* | E* | E* | | | |
| 10) Felis wiedii<br>   Margay | | | | | | | | | | | | | | | | | | E* | | | |
| 11) Reithrodontomys raviventris<br>   Mouse, Harvest, Salt Marsh | | | | | | | | | | | | | | | | | | | E | | |

116

| MAMMALS (Cont.) | ME | NH | MA | RI | CT | NY | NJ | DE | MD | VA | NC | SC | GA | FL | AL | MS | LA | TX | CA | OR | WA |
|---|---|---|---|---|---|---|---|---|---|---|---|---|---|---|---|---|---|---|---|---|---|
| 12) Felis pardalis Ocelot | | | | | | | | | | | | | | | | | E* | E | | | |
| 13) Enhydra lutris nereis Otter, Sea, Southern | | | | | | | | | | | | | | | | | | | T | T | T |
| 14) Felis concolor coryi Panther, Florida | | | | | | | | | | | | E* | E* | E | E | E | E | | | | |
| 15) Dipodomys heermanni morroensis Rat, Kangaroo Morro Bay | | | | | | | | | | | | | | | | | | | E | | |
| 16) Monachus tropicalis Seal, Monk, Caribbean (West Indian) | | | | | | | | | | | | | | E* | | | | | | | |
| 17) Sciurus niger cinereus Squirrel, Fox, Delmarva Peninsula | | | | | | | | E* | E | E | | | | | | | | | | | |
| 18) Balaenoptera musculus Whale, Blue | E | E | E | E | E | E | E | E | E | E | E | E | E | E | | | | | E | E | E |
| 19) Balaenoptera physalus Whale, Finback | E | E | E | E | E | E | E | E | E | E | E | E | E | E | | | | | E | E | E |
| 20) Eschrichtius gibbosus Whale, Gray | E* | E* | E* | E* | E* | E* | E* | E* | E* | E* | E* | E* | E* | E* | | | | | E | E | E |
| 21) Megaptera novaeangliae Whale, Humpback | E | E | E | E | E | E | E | E | E | E | E | E | E | E | | | | | E | E | E |
| 22) Eubalaena spp. Whale, Right | E | E | E | E | E | E | E | E | E | E | E | E | E | E | | | | | E | E | E |
| 23) Balaenoptera borealis Whale, Sei | E | E | E | E | E | E | E | E | E | E | E | E | E | E | | | | | E | E | E |
| 24) Physeter catodon Whale, Sperm | E | E | E | E | E | E | E | E | E | E | E | E | E | E | | | | | E | E | E |

117

| MAMMALS (Cont.) | ME | NH | MA | RI | CT | NY | NJ | DE | MD | VA | NC | SC | GA | FL | AL | MS | LA | TX | CA | OR | WA |
|---|---|---|---|---|---|---|---|---|---|---|---|---|---|---|---|---|---|---|---|---|---|
| 25) Canis lupus — Wolf, Gray | E* | E* | E* | E* | E* | E* | E* | E* | E* | E* | E* | E* | E* |  |  |  |  | E* |  | E* | E* |
| 26) Canis rufus — Wolf, Red |  |  |  |  |  |  |  |  |  |  |  |  |  | E* | E* | E* | E* | E* |  |  |  |
| **BIRDS** | | | | | | | | | | | | | | | | | | | | | |
| 1) Gymnogyps californianus — Condor, California |  |  |  |  |  |  |  |  |  |  |  |  |  |  |  |  |  |  | E | E* |  |
| 2) Grus canadensis pulla — Crane, Sandhill, Mississippi |  |  |  |  |  |  |  |  |  |  |  |  |  |  |  | E |  |  |  |  |  |
| 3) Grus americana — Crane, Whooping |  |  |  |  |  |  |  |  |  |  |  |  |  |  |  |  | E* | E |  |  |  |
| 4) Numenius borealis — Curlew, Eskimo | E* | E* | E* | E* | E* | E* | E* | E* | E* | E* | E* | E* | E* | E* |  |  | E* | E* |  |  |  |
| 5) Haliaeetus leucocephalus — Eagle, Bald | E | E | E | E | E | E | E | E | E | E | E | E | E | E | E | E | E | E | E | T | T |
| 6) Falco peregrinus anatum — Falcon, Peregrine, American | E* | E* | E* | E* | E* | E* | E* | E* | E* | E* | E* | E* | E* | E* | E* | E* | E* | E | E | E | E |
| 7) Falco peregrinus tundrius — Falcon, Peregrine, Artic | E | E | E | E | E | E | E | E | E | E | E | E | E | E | E | E | E | E | E | E | E |
| 8) Branta canadensis leucopareia — Goose, Canada, Aleutian |  |  |  |  |  |  |  |  |  |  |  |  |  |  |  |  |  |  | E | E |  |
| 9) Rostrhamus sociabilis plumbeus — Kite, Florida Everglade (Snail Hawk) |  |  |  |  |  |  |  |  |  |  |  |  |  | E |  |  |  |  |  |  |  |

# BIRDS (Cont.)

| | ME | NH | MA | RI | CT | NY | NJ | DE | MD | VA | NC | SC | GA | FL | AL | MS | LA | TX | CA | OR | WA |
|---|---|---|---|---|---|---|---|---|---|---|---|---|---|---|---|---|---|---|---|---|---|
| 10) Pelecanus occidentalis<br>Pelican, Brown | | | | | | | | | | E* | E | E | E | E | E | E | E | E | E | E | E |
| 11) Tympanuchus cupido attwateri<br>Prairie chicken, Greater, Attwater's | | | | | | | | | | | | | | | | | E* | E | | | |
| 12) Rallus longirostris obsoletus<br>Rail, Clapper, California | | | | | | | | | | | | | | | | | | | E | | |
| 13) Rallus longirostris levipes<br>Rail, Clapper, Light-Footed | | | | | | | | | | | | | | | | | | | E | | |
| 14) Lanius ludovicianus mearnsi<br>Shrike, Loggerhead, San Clemente | | | | | | | | | | | | | | | | | | | E | | |
| 15) Ammospiza maritima mirabilis<br>Sparrow, Cape Sable | | | | | | | | | | | | | | E | | | | | | | |
| 16) Amphispiza belli clementae<br>Sparrow, Sage, San Clemente | | | | | | | | | | | | | | | | | | | T | | |
| 17) Ammospiza maritima nigrescens<br>Sparrow, Seaside, Dusky | | | | | | | | | | | | | | E | | | | | | | |
| 18) Melospiza melodia graminea<br>Sparrow, Song, Santa Barbara | | | | | | | | | | | | | | | | | | | E* | | |
| 19) Sterna albifrons browni<br>Tern, Least, California | | | | | | | | | | | | | | | | | | | E | | |
| 20) Vermivora bachmanii<br>Warbler Bachman's | | | | | | | | | | E* | E* | E* | E* | E* | E* | E* | E* | | | | |
| 21) Campephilus principalis<br>Woodpecker, Ivory-Billed | | | | | | | | | | E* | E* | E* | E* | E* | E* | E* | E* | E* | | | |

119

BIRDS (Cont.)

| | ME | NH | MA | RI | CT | NY | NJ | DE | MD | VA | NC | SC | GA | FL | AL | MS | LA | TX | CA | OR | WA |
|---|----|----|----|----|----|----|----|----|----|----|----|----|----|----|----|----|----|----|----|----|----|
| 22) Picoides (Dendrocopus) borealis Woodpecker, Red-Cockaded | | | | | | | | E | E | E | E | E | E | E | E | E | E | E | | | |

PLANTS

| | ME | NH | MA | RI | CT | NY | NJ | DE | MD | VA | NC | SC | GA | FL | AL | MS | LA | TX | CA | OR | WA |
|---|----|----|----|----|----|----|----|----|----|----|----|----|----|----|----|----|----|----|----|----|----|
| 1) Arabis macdonaldiana Rockcress, Mc Donald's | | | | | | | | | | | | | | | | | | | E | | |
| 2) Erysimum capitatum var. angustatum Wallflower, Contra Costa | | | | | | | | | | | | | | | | | | | E | | |
| 3) Echinocereus reichenbachii var. albertii Cactus, Black Lace | | | | | | | | | | | | | | | | | | E | | | |
| 4) Dudleya traskiae Liveforever, Santa Barbara Island | | | | | | | | | | | | | | | | | | | E | | |
| 5) Arctostaphylos hookeri ssp. ravenii Manzanita, Raven's (Presidio) | | | | | | | | | | | | | | | | | | | E | | |
| 6) Rhododendron chapmanii (minus var. chapmanii) Rhododendron, Chapman | | | | | | | | | | | | | | E | | | | | | | |
| 7) Lotus scoparius ssp. traskiae Broom, San Clemente | | | | | | | | | | | | | | | | | | | E | | |
| 8) Pogogyne abramsii Pogogyne, San Diego | | | | | | | | | | | | | | | | | | | E | | |
| 9) Harperocallis flava Harper's Beauty | | | | | | | | | | | | | | E | | | | | | | |
| 10) Malacothamnus clementinus Bushmallow, San Clemente Island | | | | | | | | | | | | | | | | | | | E | | |

120

PLANTS (Cont.)

| | ME | NH | MA | RI | CT | NY | NJ | DE | MD | VA | NC | SC | GA | FL | AL | MS | LA | TX | CA | OR | WA |
|---|---|---|---|---|---|---|---|---|---|---|---|---|---|---|---|---|---|---|---|---|---|
| 11) Oenothera deltoides ssp. howellii Evening-Primrose, Antioch Dunes | | | | | | | | | | | | | | | | | | | E | | |
| 12) Orcuttia mucronata Grass, Orcutt, Crampton's | | | | | | | | | | | | | | | | | | | E | | |
| 13) Delphinium kinkiense Larkspur, San Clemente Island | | | | | | | | | | | | | | | | | | | E | | |
| 14) Castilleja grisea (hololeuca ssp. grisea) Indian Paintbrush, San Clemente Island | | | | | | | | | | | | | | | | | | | E | | |
| 15) Cordylanthus maritimus ssp. maritimus Bird's-Beak, Salt Marsh | | | | | | | | | | | | | | | | | | | E | E* | |

REPTILES

| | ME | NH | MA | RI | CT | NY | NJ | DE | MD | VA | NC | SC | GA | FL | AL | MS | LA | TX | CA | OR | WA |
|---|---|---|---|---|---|---|---|---|---|---|---|---|---|---|---|---|---|---|---|---|---|
| 1) Alligator mississippiensis Alligator, American | | | | | | | | | | | E | B | T | | E | E | T | B | | | |
| 2) Crocodylus acutus Crocodile, American | | | | | | | | | | | | | | E | | | | | | | |
| 3) Crotaphytus silus Lizard, Leopard, Blunt-nosed | | | | | | | | | | | | | | | | | | | E | | |
| 4) Klauberina riversiana Lizard, Night, Island | | | | | | | | | | | | | | | | | | | T | | |
| 5) Thamnophis sirtalis tetrataenia Snake, Garte., San Francisco | | | | | | | | | | | | | | | | | | | E | | |
| 6) Drymarchon corais couperi Snake, Indigo, Eastern | | | | | | | | | | | | T* | T | T | T* | T* | | | | | |

121

## REPTILES (Cont.)

| | ME | NH | MA | RI | CT | NY | NJ | DE | MD | VA | NC | SC | GA | FL | AL | MS | LA | TX | CA | OR | WA |
|---|---|---|---|---|---|---|---|---|---|---|---|---|---|---|---|---|---|---|---|---|---|
| 7) Nerodia (Natrix) fasciata taeniata Snake, Water-, Salt Marsh, Atlantic | | | | | | | | | | | | | | T | | | | | | | |
| 8) Chelonia mydas Turtle, Sea, Green | | | T | T | T | T | T | T | T | T | T | T | T | E | T | T | T | T | T | T | T |
| 9) Eretmochelys imbricata Turtle, Sea, Hawksbill | | | E | E | E | E | E | E | E | E | E | E | E | E | E | E | E | E | E | E | E |
| 10) Dermochelys coriacea Turtle, Sea, Leatherback | | | E | E | E | E | E | E | E | E | E | E | E | E | E | E | E | E | E | E | E |
| 11) Caretta caretta Turtle, Sea, Loggerhead | | | T | T | T | T | T | T | T | T | T | T | T | T | T | T | T | T | T | T | T |
| 12) Lepidochelys kempii Turtle, Sea, Ridley, Kemp's (Atlantic) | | | E | E | E | E | E | E | E | E | E | E | E | E | E | E | E | E | E | E | E |
| 13) Lepidochelys olivacea Turtle, Sea, Ridley, Olive (Pacific) | | | T | T | T | T | T | T | T | T | T | T | T | T | T | T | T | T | T | T | T |

## INSECTS

| | ME | NH | MA | RI | CT | NY | NJ | DE | MD | VA | NC | SC | GA | FL | AL | MS | LA | TX | CA | OR | WA |
|---|---|---|---|---|---|---|---|---|---|---|---|---|---|---|---|---|---|---|---|---|---|
| 1) Shijimiaeoides battoides allyni Butterfly, Blue, El Segundo | | | | | | | | | | | | | | | | | | | E | | |
| 2) Lycaeides argyrognomon lotis Butterfly, Blue, Lotis | | | | | | | | | | | | | | | | | | | E | | |
| 3) Icaricia icarioides missionensis Butterfly, Blue, Mission | | | | | | | | | | | | | | | | | | | E | | |
| 4) Pseudophilotes enoptes smithi Butterfly, Blue, Smith's | | | | | | | | | | | | | | | | | | | E | | |

INSECTS (Cont.)

| | ME | NH | MA | RI | CT | NY | NJ | DE | MD | VA | NC | SC | GA | FL | AL | MS | LA | TX | CA | OR | WA |
|---|---|---|---|---|---|---|---|---|---|---|---|---|---|---|---|---|---|---|---|---|---|
| 5) Callophrys mossii bayensis<br>Butterfly, Elfin, San Bruno | | | | | | | | | | | | | | | | | | | E | | |
| 6) Apodemia mormo langei<br>Butterfly, Metalmark, Lange's | | | | | | | | | | | | | | | | | | | E | | |
| 7) Papilio andraemon bonhotei<br>Butterfly, Swallowtail, Bahama | | | | | | | | | | | | | | T | | | | | | | |
| 8) Papilio aristodemus ponceanus<br>Butterfly, Swallowtail, Schaus' | | | | | | | | | | | | | | T | | | | | | | |

FISH

| | ME | NH | MA | RI | CT | NY | NJ | DE | MD | VA | NC | SC | GA | FL | AL | MS | LA | TX | CA | OR | WA |
|---|---|---|---|---|---|---|---|---|---|---|---|---|---|---|---|---|---|---|---|---|---|
| 1) Etheostoma sellare<br>Darter, Maryland | | | | | | | | | E | | | | | | | | | | | | |
| 2) Etheostoma okaloosae<br>Darter, Okaloosa | | | | | | | | | | | | | | E | | | | | | | |
| 3) Gasterosteus aculeatus williamsoni<br>Stickleback, Threespine, Unarmored | | | | | | | | | | | | | | | | | | | E | | |
| 4) Acipenser brevirostrum<br>Sturgeon, Shortnose | E | E | E | E | E | E | E | E | E | E | E | E | E | E | | | | | | | |

AMPHIBIANS

| | ME | NH | MA | RI | CT | NY | NJ | DE | MD | VA | NC | SC | GA | FL | AL | MS | LA | TX | CA | OR | WA |
|---|---|---|---|---|---|---|---|---|---|---|---|---|---|---|---|---|---|---|---|---|---|
| 1) Hyla andersonii<br>Frog, Tree-, Pine Barrens, (Florida population) | | | | | | | | | | | | | | E | | | | | | | |
| 2) Ambystoma macrodactylum croceum<br>Salamander, Long-Toed, Santa Cruz | | | | | | | | | | | | | | | | | | | E | | |

## AMPHIBIANS (Cont.)

| | ME | NH | MA | RI | CT | NY | NJ | DE | MD | VA | NC | SC | GA | FL | AL | MS | LA | TX | CA | OR | WA |
|---|----|----|----|----|----|----|----|----|----|----|----|----|----|----|----|----|----|----|----|----|----|
| 3) Bufo houstonensis Toad, Houston | | | | | | | | | | | | | | | | | | E | | | |

### SNAILS

| | ME | NH | MA | RI | CT | NY | NJ | DE | MD | VA | NC | SC | GA | FL | AL | MS | LA | TX | CA | OR | WA |
|---|----|----|----|----|----|----|----|----|----|----|----|----|----|----|----|----|----|----|----|----|----|
| 1) Orthalicus reses Snail, Tree, Stock Island | | | | | | | | | | | | | | E | | | | | | | |

### CLAMS

NO LISTED SPECIES FOR COASTAL COUNTIES OF CONTERMINOUS U.S.

### CRUSTACEANS

NO LISTED SPECIES FOR COASTAL COUNTIES OF CONTERMINOUS U.S.

### OTHERS

NO LISTED SPECIES FOR COASTAL COUNTIES OF CONTERMINOUS U.S.

124

# VIII NATURAL AREAS

Coastal county nonmetropolitan population growth outstripped other population growth between 1960 and 1976 (see the tables and figures in Section II). Population growth in these areas places demands on the development of the more natural areas of the coast. These natural areas provide not only for the preservation of wildlife, but also for recreational opportunities for millions of people. In this section, we show the results of federal efforts, as well as the efforts of two private groups to conserve natural areas in the coast. Although the amounts preserved seem large--4.6 million acres of federal coastal property, and nearly 200,000 acres of private conservancy property--these acres are less than 4% of the total area of the coastal counties.

# 41. NATIONAL PARKS

The enabling legislation of the National Park System (1916) establishes the purpose of the service "to conserve the scenery and the natural and historic objects therein and to provide for the enjoyment of the same in such manner and by such means as will leave them unimpaired for future generations."

Of the 321 units in the National Park System, 41 are on the Atlantic Gulf and Pacific Coasts of the contiguous 48 states. These areas occupy over 3.4 million acres and were visited by over 65 million people in 1978. The recent trend shows an annual increase in visitation of 6.5% annually.

The gasoline shortage of 1979 led to a decrease in visits to the National Park system of 7.6%. The trend through 1978 had suggested that coastal park visitation would double in the next 11 years, but future increases are dependent on the availability of gasoline. Even with reduced energy use, the coastal parks will remain a public recreation resource of major significance.

The acronyms describing each park type are given in full name in Table 41c.

Table 41a.  COASTAL NATIONAL PARKS, ACREAGE AND VISITATION.

| | Acres | 1978 Visitors (in thousands) | Average Annual % Increase 1970-1978 |
|---|---|---|---|
| Acadia NP, ME | 38,631 | 3,130.0 | 1.4 |
| Assateague Island NS, MD-VA | 39,631 | 2,135.9 | 2.9 |
| Biscayne NM, FL | 103,642 | 177.4 | 9.3 [1] |
| Boston NHP, MA | --- | 2,749.0 | -- [9] |
| Cabrillo NM, CA | 144 | 1,338.2 | 0.8 |
| Canaveral NS, FL | 57,627 | 882.6 | 9.4 [5] |
| Cape Cod NS, MA | 44,596 | 5,025.9 | 2.6 |
| Cape Hatteras, NS, NC | 30,319 | 2,043.3 | 5.0 |
| Cape Lookout NS, NC | 28,400 | 54.3 | 16.4 [6] |
| Castillo De San Marcos NM, FL | 20 | 774.6 | 4.2 |
| Channel Islands NP, CA | 124,740 | 56.1 | 5.4 |
| Colonial NHP, VA | 9,462 | 10,804.2 | 2.4 |
| Cumberland Island NS, GA | 36,978 | 36.4 | 25.6 [5] |
| De Soto NMe, FL | 30 | 142.2 | 0.7 |
| Everglades NP, FL | 1,398,800 | 1,136.1 | -1.5 |
| Fire Island NS, NY | 19,579 | 637.1 | 3.9 |
| Ft. Caroline NMe, FL | 139 | 168.0 | 6.8 |
| Ft. Clatsop NMe, OR | 130 | 88.7 | -3.8 |
| Ft. Frederica NM, GA | 214 | 42.0 | 5.4 |
| Ft. Jefferson NM, FL | 47,125 | 18.7 | 3.9 |
| Ft. Matanzas NM, FL | 299 | 293.5 | 4.3 |
| Ft. McHenry NM, MD | 43 | 527.8 | -1.0 |
| Ft. Point NHS, CA | 29 | 806.0 | 6.1 [1] |
| Ft. Pulaski NM, GA | 5,615 | 348.9 | 3.9 |

Table 41a.  COASTAL NATIONAL PARKS, ACREAGE AND VISITATION (cont.)

| | Acres | 1978 Visitors (in thousands) | Average Annual % Increase 1970-1978 |
|---|---|---|---|
| Ft. Raleigh NHS, NC | 157 | 349.2 | 2.2 |
| Ft. Sumter NM, SC | 64 | 204.9 | 1.7 |
| Gateway NRA, NY-NJ | 26,172 | 9,017.5 | 3.4[4] |
| Golden Gate NRA, CA | 38,677 | 8,960.9 | 23.0[3] |
| Gulf Islands NS, FL-MS | 139,775 | 3,971.6 | 15.2[2] |
| Jean Lafitte NHP, LA | 20,000 | 304.5[7] | 1.7 |
| Mar-A-Lago NHS, FL | 17 | ---[7] | --[7] |
| Olympic NP, WA | 908,781 | 2,996.6 | 3.0 |
| Padre Island NS, TX | 133,918 | 867.0 | 2.1 |
| Point Reyes NS, CA | 67,265 | 1,945.8 | 5.5 |
| Redwood NP, CA | 109,028 | 513.4 | 8.6 |
| St. Croix Island NM, Me | 35 | --- | --[2] |
| Sagamore Hill NHS, NY | 78 | 187.3 | 2.7 |
| Salem Maritime NHS, MA | 9 | 300.2 | .5 |
| San Juan Island NHP, WA | 1,752 | 76.4 | 9.5 |
| Statue of Liberty NM, NY-NJ | 58 | 1,507.9 | 3.3 |
| Wright Brothers NM, NC | 431 | 483.5 | -.2 |

Table 41b.  COASTAL NATIONAL PARKS SIZE AND VISITS BY REGION.

| | # Areas | Acreage | Visitors (in thousands) | Average Annual % Increase 1970-1978 |
|---|---|---|---|---|
| Atlantic | 26 | 442,216 | 41,881.4 | 3.0 |
| Gulf | 6 | 1,739,648 | 6,440.1 | 9.5 |
| Pacific | 9 | 1,250,546 | 16,782.1 | 14.1 |
| All | 41 | 3,432,410 | 65,103.6 | 6.7 |

---

[1] first data 1972
[2] first data 1973
[3] first data 1974
[4] first data 1975
[5] first data 1976
[6] first data 1977
[7] not open to public
[8] no Federal facilities
[9] first data 1978

Table 41c.  COASTAL NATIONAL PARKS -- SIZE AND VISITS BY CLASS OF PARK.

| | # Areas | Acreage | Visitor in (thousands) | Average Annual % Increase 1970-1978 |
|---|---|---|---|---|
| National Park (NP) | 5 | 2,579,980 | 7,832.2 | 2.1 |
| National Seashore (NS) | 10 | 598,088 | 17,599.9 | 6.5 |
| National Monument (NM) | 12 | 157,690 | 5,717.4 | 2.4 |
| National Historic Park (NHP) | 4 | 22,214 | 13,934.1 | 2.4 |
| National Memorial (NMe) | 3 | 299 | 398.9 | 2.3 |
| National Recreation Area (NRA) | 2 | 64,849 | 17,978.4 | 13.2 |
| National Historic Site (NHS) | 5 | 290 | 1,642.7 | 3.9 |

Source adapted from:  U.S. Department of the Interior, National Park Service. 1971, 1973, 1975, 1976.  Public Use of the National Parks, annual report;                                    .
1978.  National Park Statistical Abstract.

# 42. NATIONAL WILDLIFE REFUGES

The National Wildlife Refuge System was established in 1965.[1]  Wildlife Refuges are the product of legislation which consolidated the authority of the Department of the Interior to administer lands for the conservation of fish and wildlife, including habitats of threatened or endangered species. As of 1978 over 100 refuges containing over 1 million acres have been acquired for this purpose in the coastal area.  Florida, with 17, has the most coastal refuges.  These refuges, in addition to providing sanctuary for wildlife, serve as parks.  There were over 13 million visits to coastal refuges in 1978.

[1] U.S. House of Representatives, Committee on Merchant Marine and Fisheries. 1972.  A Compilation of Federal Laws relating to Conservation and Development of our Nation's Fish and Wildlife Resources, Environmental Quality, and Oceanography.  pp. 36-37.

Table 42a. NATIONAL WILDLIFE REFUGES -- ACQUISITION COSTS AND ACREAGE
BY STATE.

| State | Total Number of Refuges | Number of Coastal Refuges | Acquisition Costs of Coastal Refuges (in thousands) | Area of Coastal Refuges (in acres) |
|---|---|---|---|---|
| Maine | 6 | 6 | 1,118 | 26,661 |
| New Hampshire | 1 | 0 | --- | --- |
| Massachusetts | 7 | 6 | 889 | 10,783 |
| Rhode Island | 4 | 4 | 0 | 543 |
| Connecticut | 1 | 1 | 2 | 183 |
| New York | 9 | 7 | 178 | 5,681 |
| New Jersey | 4 | 4 | 9,528 | 35,430 |
| Delaware | 2 | 2 | 3,891 | 24,062 |
| Maryland | 5 | 4 | 3,171 | 21,391 |
| Virginia | 8 | 5 | 260 | 23,695 |
| North Carolina | 8 | 5 | 839 | 90,304 |
| South Carolina | 5 | 3 | 893 | 53,371 |
| Georgia | 8 | 6 | 824 | 35,100 |
| Florida | 21 | 17 | 10,237 | 277,033 |
| Alabama | 4 | 0 | --- | --- |
| Mississippi | 6 | 1 | 7,335 | 8,814 |
| Louisiana | 7 | 5 | 285 | 232,478 |
| Texas | 11 | 6 | 10,158 | 164,317 |
| California | 21 | 6 | 4,613 | 17,009 |
| Oregon | 16 | 4 | 469 | 8,836 |
| Washington | 16 | 9 | 4,019 | 16,219 |
| TOTAL | 170 | 101 | 58,707 | 1,051,910 |

Source: U.S. Department of the Interior, Fish and Wildlife Service.
Annual Report of Lands under control of the U.S. Fish and
Wildlife Service as of September 30, 1978.

129

Table 42b.  NATIONAL WILDLIFE REFUGES -- VISITS BY STATE.

| State | Visits for Consumptive Wildlife Recreation[1] | Total Visits | No. Refuges Reporting | No. Coastal Refuges |
|---|---|---|---|---|
| Maine | 4,537 | 33,775 | 2 | 6 |
| New Hampshire | --- | --- | 0 | 0 |
| Massachusetts | 105,612 | 1,280,362 | 4 | 6 |
| Rhode Island | 6,591 | 47,121 | 4 | 4 |
| Connecticut | 0 | 400 | 1 | 1 |
| New York | 13 | 5,421 | 1 | 7 |
| New Jersey | 25,806 | 322,358 | 2 | 4 |
| Delaware | 6,997 | 87,965 | 2 | 2 |
| Maryland | 12,222 | 145,646 | 2 | 4 |
| Virginia | 489,626 | 1,767,765 | 3 | 5 |
| North Carolina | 187,533 | 1,532,741 | 4 | 5 |
| South Carolina | 12,661 | 53,496 | 1 | 3 |
| Georgia | 30,431 | 58,016 | 6 | 6 |
| Florida | 714,194 | 7,078,804 | 10 | 17 |
| Alabama | --- | --- | 0 | 0 |
| Mississippi | --- | --- | 0 | 1 |
| Louisiana | 53,704 | 67,830 | 4 | 5 |
| Texas | 62,281 | 652,458 | 5 | 6 |
| California | 0 | 1,346 | 3 | 6 |
| Oregon | 3,300 | 12,772 | 3 | 4 |
| Washington | 36,633 | 629,536 | 6 | 9 |
| TOTAL | 1,913,141 | 13,777,812 | 62 | 101 |

Table 42c.  NATIONAL WILDLIFE REFUGES -- VISITS BY REGION

| Region | Visits for Consumptive Wildlife Recreation | Total Visits | No. Refuges Reporting | No. Coastal Refuges |
|---|---|---|---|---|
| Maine to Virginia | 651,404 | 3,690,813 | 21 | 39 |
| North Carolina to Texas | 1,060,804 | 9,443,345 | 30 | 43 |
| Pacific | 39,933 | 643,654 | 11 | 19 |

[1] includes hunting, fishing, clamming, crabbing, and other

Source:   U.S. Department of the Interior, Fish and Wildlife Service.
          National Wildlife Refuge--Public Use Report--Visits--FY '78.

# 42d. ENDANGERED SPECIES

The conservation of species threatened with extinction is a primary goal of the National Wildlife Refuge System.  This table displays the states which have a coastal refuge reporting the occurence of a given endangered species.  In contrast, table 40 gives the state-by-state breakdown of endangered species in the coastal counties.  Because the National Wildlife Refuge list of endangered species is not an exhaustive list of species actually on the refuges, the comparison of the lists shows the absence of many endangered species that occur in coastal counties from the coastal National Wildlife Refuges.  Additionally, some of these species may not occur within a coastal National Wildlife Refuge.

Table 42d.   ENDANGERED AND THREATENED SPECIES REPORTED ON NATIONAL WILDLIFE REFUGES.

| Species | States with the Species on a Coastal National Wildlife Refuge |
|---|---|
| American Alligator (T-Threatened) | GA, FL, LA, TX |
| American Alligator | NC, SC |
| American Crocodile | FL |
| Atlantic Ridley Turtle | MA, GA, FL |
| Attwaters Greater Prairie Chicken | TX |
| Bald Eagle (T) | OR, WA |
| Bald Eagle | ME, MA, RI, NJ, DE, MD, VA, NC, SC, GA, FL, TX, CA |
| California Brown Pelican | CA, OR, WA |
| California Least Tern | CA |
| Columbian White-tailed Deer | OR, WA |
| Delmarva Peninsula Fox Squirrel | MD, VA |
| Dusky Seaside Sparrow | FL, |
| Eastern Brown Pelican | NC, SC, GA, FL, TX |
| Eastern Indigo Snake (T) | FL |
| Everglade Kite | FL |
| Florida Manatee | FL |
| Florida Panther | FL |
| Green Sea Turtle (T) | FL |
| Hawksbill Turtle | FL |
| Humpback Whale | CA |
| Jaguarundi | TX |
| Key Deer | FL |
| Leatherback Sea Turtle | MA, FL |
| Light-footed Clapper Rail | CA |
| Loggerhead Sea Turtle (T) | MD, VA, NC, SC, GA, FL |
| Mississippi Sandhill Crane | MS |
| Ocelot | TX |
| Peregrine Falcon | ME, MA, NJ, DE, VA, NC, GA, FL, LA, TX, CA, OR, WA |
| Red-cockaded Woodpecker | MD, VA, NC, GA, FL |
| Red Wolf | LA, TX |
| Santa Cruz Long-Toed Salamander | CA |
| Whooping Crane | TX |

Source:   U.S. Fish and Wildlife Service; Memorandum from the Associate Director, Wildlife Resources, U.S. Fish and Wildlife Service, June 7, 1979.

# 43. PRIVATE CONSERVANCIES

Private groups hold over 100 coastal properties for the purpose of preservation. The coastal properties of The Nature Conservancy and the Audubon Society are listed here. The largest single property is The Nature Conservancy holding on Santa Cruz Island, California which is 55,000 acres and provides habitat for seven endangered or threatened species. West coast sanctuaries account for seventeen of these sanctuaries while sanctuaries in Maine number thirty four.

One of the outstanding properties held by The Nature Conservancy is The Virginia Coastal Reserve. This reserve is 35,000 acres of 13 barrier islands off the eastern shore of Virginia. These islands are shown below.

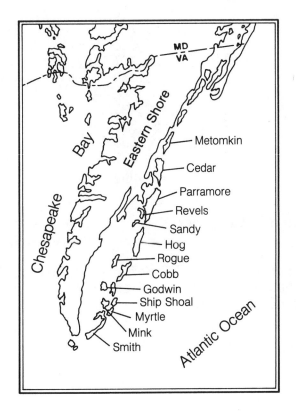

THE VIRGINIA COASTAL RESERVE. These 13 barrier islands make up the reserve which is owned by The Nature Conservancy. (from The Nature Conservancy).

Table 43.  PRIVATE CONSERVANCY HOLDINGS -- NUMBERS AND ACREAGE BY STATE.

| State | The Nature Conservancy | | Audubon Society | |
|---|---|---|---|---|
| | Number | Acres | Number | Acres |
| Maine | 28 | 2,878 | 6 | 906 |
| Connecticut | 4 | 117 | 1 | 200 |
| New York | 12 | 432 | 1 | 267 |
| Maryland | 1 | 16 | 1 | 58 |
| Virginia | 2 | 33,760 | -- | -- |
| North Carolina | 3 | 7,306 | 1 | 3,500 |
| South Carolina | 1 | 23,777 | 1 | 250 |
| Florida | 12 | 5,060 | 6 | 4,149 |
| Louisiana | -- | -- | 1 | 26,800 |
| Texas | 2 | 2,383 | 9 | 10,617 |
| California | 7 | 61,315 | 2 | 2,700 |
| Oregon | 3 | 608 | -- | -- |
| Washington | 5 | 431 | -- | -- |
| TOTAL | 80 | 138,083 | 30 | 49,553 |

Total 110 Sanctuaries
      187,636 Private Sanctuary Acres

Source:  The Nature Conservancy, 1800 North Kent Street, Arlington, VA,
         22209; The National Audubon Society Sanctuary Director, Miles
         Wildlife Sanctuary, West Cornwall Road, Sharon, CT, 06069.

# 44. ESTUARINE SANCTUARIES

The Estuarine Sanctuaries system operated by the Coastal Zone Management Office of The National Oceanic and Atmospheric Administration (Department of Commerce) is the only federal program directed exclusively to the nation's estuaries. The five listed below are the only seacoast sanctuaries in the coterminous United States. The authorizing legislation for Estuarine Sanctuaries was passed in October, 1972. The Sanctuaries are established and added to the system for the purpose of providing "living laboratories" for scientific research, and public education to be operated by the individual states.

Table 44. FEDERAL ESTUARINE SANCTUARIES -- LOCATIONS AND SIZES.[1,2]

| Name and Location | Acreage |
|---|---|
| Sapelo Island<br>McIntosh County, Georgia | 7,400 |
| South Slough<br>Coos Bay, Coos County, Oregon | 4,200 |
| Rookery Bay<br>Collier County, Florida | 8,500 |
| Apalachicola River/Bay<br>Franklin County, Florida | 193,000 |
| Elkhorn Slough<br>Monterey County, California | 1,510 |

[1] Source: U.S. Department of Commerce, NOAA, Estuarine Sanctuary Program
[2] Additional Federal Estuarine Sanctuaries are located in Hawaii, (5900 acres) and, Ohio (637 acres).

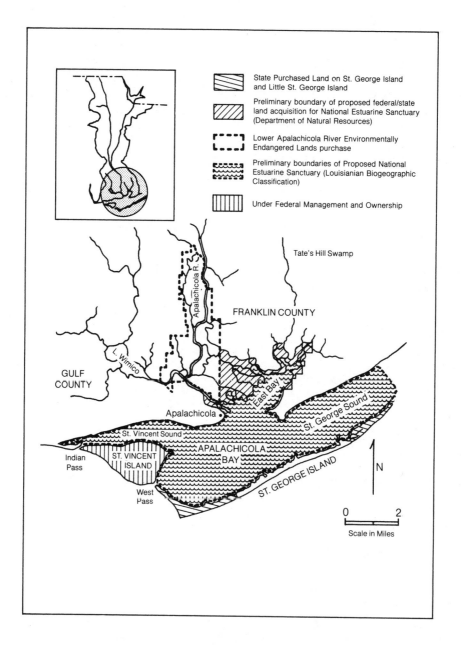

Legend:

- State Purchased Land on St. George Island and Little St. George Island
- Preliminary boundary of proposed federal/state land acquisition for National Estuarine Sanctuary (Department of Natural Resources)
- Lower Apalachicola River Environmentally Endangered Lands purchase
- Preliminary boundaries of Proposed National Estuarine Sanctuary (Louisianian Biogeographic Classification)
- Under Federal Management and Ownership

Tate's Hill Swamp

Apalachicola R.

FRANKLIN COUNTY

L. Wimico

GULF COUNTY

Apalachicola

East Bay

St. George Sound

St. Vincent Sound

Indian Pass

ST. VINCENT ISLAND

APALACHICOLA BAY

ST. GEORGE ISLAND

West Pass

N

0    2
Scale in Miles

APALACHICOLA BAY ESTUARINE SANCTUARY. This sanctuary is the nation's largest. It occupies over 300 square miles in the Florida panhandle. (from Florida Department of Administration, Division of State Planning, Bureau of Land and Water Management, April, 1977. The Apalachicola River and Bay System: A Florida Resource.)

# IX RECREATION

The nation's ocean beaches and waters and its estuaries, sounds and bays comprise an enormous recreational asset. Millions of saltwater fishermen spend billions of dollars and many days fishing every year. Millions of others swim or boat in the coastal area. The continued ability of these people to enjoy the coast depends upon their ease of access to aesthetically pleasing areas where they can find waters whose quality exceeds certain minimal requirements and which contain a reasonable abundance of desirable fishes.

# 45. RECREATIONAL FISHING

Twenty-two million fishermen spent 4.5 billion dollars on saltwater recreational fishing in 1975. As can be seen in the accompanying figure, a dramatic increase in these expenditures has occurred since 1955. Tables 45a, b, and c describe participation and economic aspects of recreational fishing (Tables 37 and 38 summarize the catch of these fishermen.)

Table 45a. SALTWATER RECREATIONAL FISHING -- PARTICIPATION AND EXPENSES.

|  | Number of Fishermen[1] | Expenditures[f] | Number of days of Participation | Passenger Miles |
|---|---|---|---|---|
| 1955 | 4,557,000 | 488,939,000 | 58,621,000 | 2,904,001,000 |
| 1960 | 6,292,000 | 626,191,000 | 80,602,000 | 3,404,945,000 |
| 1965 | 8,305,000 | 799,656,000 | 95,837,000 | 4,138,307,000 |
| 1970 | 9,460,000 | 1,224,705,000 | 113,694,000 | 5,459,276,000 |
| 1975[b] | 16,307,000 | 3,450,358,000 | 207,212,000 | a |
| 1975[c] | 22,687,000 | 4,508,311,000 | 260,617,000 | a |
| 1975[d] | 25,372,000 |  | 240,019,000 |  |

Table 45b. SALTWATER RECREATIONAL FISHING -- PER CAPITA ACTIVITY.

|  | Expenditures Per Participant[f] | Days of Participation Per Fisherman | Automobile Miles Per Fisherman |
|---|---|---|---|
| 1955 | 107 | 12.9 | 637 |
| 1960 | 100 | 12.8 | 541 |
| 1965 | 96 | 11.5 | 498 |
| 1970 | 129 | 12.0 | 577 |
| 1975[b] | 212 | 12.7 | a |
| 1975[c] | 199 | 11.5 | a |
| 1975[d] | a | 9.5 | a |

FISHING ON BIRD SHOAL, NORTH CAROLINA. (Following Page) This angler is trying his luck on Bird Shoal. This island near Beaufort, North Carolina, was preserved by the efforts of The Nature Conservancy in conjunction with the local citizenry. (Photo by Irving Hooper)

Table 45c.   SALTWATER RECREATIONAL FISHING -- CONSTANT DOLLAR EXPENDITURES
(ADJUSTED TO THE 1972 DOLLAR).

|  | Expenditures | Expenditures Per Fisherman |
|---|---|---|
| 1955 | 801,802,000 | 175.9 |
| 1960 | 911,884,000 | 144.9 |
| 1965 | 1,075,963,000 | 129.6 |
| 1970 | 1,340,526,000 | 141.7 |
| 1975[b] | 2,711,479,000 | 166.3 |
| 1975[c] | 3,542,877,000 | 156.2 |
| 1975[d] | a | a |

---

[1] The definition of a fisherman varied from year to year.  This table
outlines those differences.

| A fisherman includes | 1975 | 1970 | Previous to 1970 | 1955 |
|---|---|---|---|---|
| those over: | 9 yrs. old | 12 yrs. old | 12 yrs. old | 12 yrs. old |
| participating: | 1 dy. or more | 3 dys. or more | 3 dys. or more | 3 dys. or more |
| spending: | $0.00 or more | $7.50 or more | $5.00 or more | $5.00 or more |
| | | | | |
| fishing in all saltwater states: | including Alaska and Hawaii | including Alaska and Hawaii | including Alaska and Hawaii | excluding Alaska and Hawaii |

a not available
b excluding sea run fishes
c includes sea run fishes
d clamming, crabbing and shell collecting
e a fisherman had to meet either the participation or spending requirements.
f in dollars of the year indicated
Source:   U.S. Department of the Interior, Fish and Wildlife Service, Bureau
of Sport Fisheries and Wildlife; 1970 National Survey of Fishing and
Hunting, Resource Publication Number 95, 108 pp; U.S. Department of
the Interior, Fish and Wildlife Service. 1975 National Survey of
Hunting Fishing and Wildlife Associated Recreation. 98 pp;  U.S.
Department of Commerce, Bureau of the Census, Statistical Abstract
of the United States.

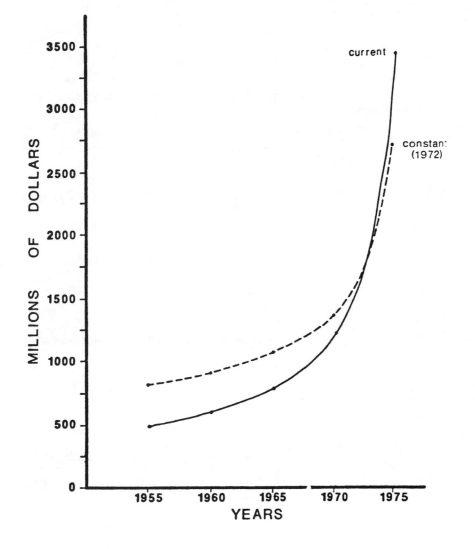

SALTWATER RECREATIONAL FISHERMEN
expenditures

Dramatic increases in fishing expenditures have occurred during the
70's even accounting for inflation.  (By Ruth Ann Hill)

141

# 46. BOATING, SWIMMING, WATER SKIING

Swimming represents one of the most popular forms of recreation at the shore. On the average, Americans swam almost five days each at the coast, and the Department of Commerce expects us to spend even more time swimming in the future. Pleasure boating and water skiing are also very popular activities. The figures here describe recreational activity in Bureau of Economic Analysis zones contiguous to the shore rather than at the shore. Since these zones are often large, these figures include some activity in noncoastal areas.

Table 46. COASTAL RECREATION -- BOATING, SWIMMING, AND WATER SKIING (DAYS IN THOUSANDS).

| Region | Boating[1] Days | % In-crease[3] | Swimming[2] Days | % In-crease[3] | Water Skiing Days | % In-crease[3] |
|---|---|---|---|---|---|---|
| New England | | | | | | |
| ME-CT | 5,551 | 20 | 35,052 | 13 | 2,203 | 20 |
| Mid-Atlantic | | | | | | |
| NY-DE | 10,688 | 23 | 71,421 | 14 | 4,189 | 26 |
| South Atlantic | | | | | | |
| MD-FL | 12,664 | 19 | 42,661 | 14 | 6,622 | 16 |
| Gulf | | | | | | |
| AL-TX | 5,539 | 18 | 19,371 | 12 | 2,962 | 14 |
| Pacific | | | | | | |
| CA-WA | 14,603 | 21 | 63,626 | 16 | 8,826 | 13 |
| TOTAL | 49,045 | 21 | 232,232 | 14 | 24,803 | 17 |

[1] other than water skiing
[2] other than pool swimming
[3] % increase expected 72-78

Source: Modified from Robert J. Kalter, Recreation Activities in the Nation's Estuarine Zone. In Estuarine Control & Assessment, Volume I. EPA. Report Number 400/1-77-007A March, 1977. Office of Water Planning and Standards, pp. 83-94. Department of Commerce, Bureau of Economic Analysis, Zones Contiguous to Shore.

SUNBATHING represents an immensely popular form of recreation. This is Miami Beach (Photo by Miami Beach Visitor and Convention Authority).

# X. HURRICANES

Hurricanes are powerful storms with winds exceeding seventy three miles per hour that lash the coasts and the interior of the United States.  In addition to their winds and rains, they may be accompanied by storm surges which can completely wash over low-lying areas.  Since Galveston was devastated by a hurricane in 1900 which killed 6,000 people, the trend has been toward reports of increased property damage, and decreased loss of life. The two major hurricanes in 1979 caused $2.6 billion in property damage and claimed ten casualties.

Hurricane season typically extends from early June through October, with a few storms in November, although one aberrant hurricane struck the coast in February.

# 47. HURRICANES

Table 47.   DAMAGES AND DEATHS FROM MAJOR HURRICANES IN THE UNITED STATES --
1954-1979.

| Name of Hurricane | Time (Month-Year) | Damages (Millions) | Deaths (Number) | Region of Losses |
|---|---|---|---|---|
| Carol | Aug 54 | $461 | 60 | Northeast |
| Hazel | Oct 54 | 281 | 95 | Southeast/ Northeast |
| Diane | Aug 55 | 832 | 184 | Northeast |
| Audrey | Jun 57 | 150 | 390 | Gulf |
| Donna | Sep 60 | 387 | 50 | Southeast/ Northeast |
| Carla | Sep 61 | 408 | 46 | Gulf |
| Betsy | Sep 65 | 1,420 | 75 | Southeast/ Gulf |
| Beulah | Sep 67 | 200 | 15 | Gulf |
| Camille | Aug 69 | 1,421 | 256 | Gulf/ Northeast |
| Celia | Aug 70 | 453 | 11 | Gulf |
| Agnes | Jun 72 | 2,100 | 122 | Northeast |
| Carmen | Sep 74 | 150 | 1 | Gulf |
| Eloise | Sep 75 | 550 | 21 | Gulf/ Northeast |
| David | Sep 79 | 320 | 5 | Southeast/ Northeast |
| Frederic | Sep 79 | 2,300 | 5 | Gulf |

Source:   Dacy and Kunreuther (1969), The Economics of Natural Disasters,
Years 1954-1965;  U.S. Army Corps of Engineers, Hurricane Reports,
1966-1978;  Platt, R. and McMillan, G. (1978), Paul Hebert,
National Hurricane Center, pers. comm.

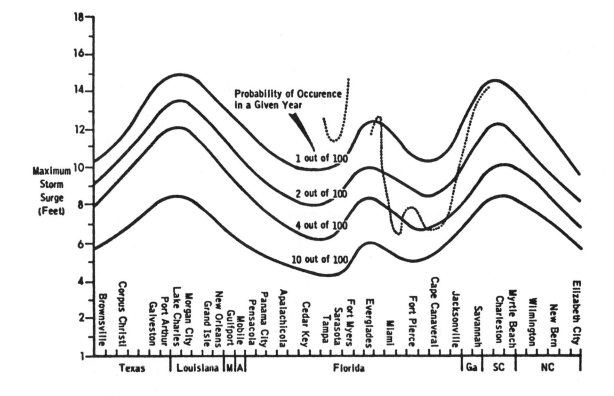

STORM SURGES often accompany hurricanes.  This figure shows the
probability of storm surges of a given height at a given location.  The
Texas-Louisiana border, the southern tip of Florida, and the coast of
South Carolina are most likely to have the highest storm surges.  The
solid lines are based on U.S. Army Corps of Engineers and University of
Florida probability estimates of annual occurrence of a storm surge on
an open beach area; dotted lines based on National Oceanic and Atmospheric
Administration data, probability of occurrence is 1 out of 100.

Note:  Greater heights are possible in bays and estuaries.  Furthermore,
about 3 feet should be added to account for wave runups, also, the effect
of the astronomical tide must be taken into consideration.  (from U.S.
Department of Commerce, NOAA, Office of Coastal Zone Management, November
1976.  Natural Hazard Management in Coastal Areas)

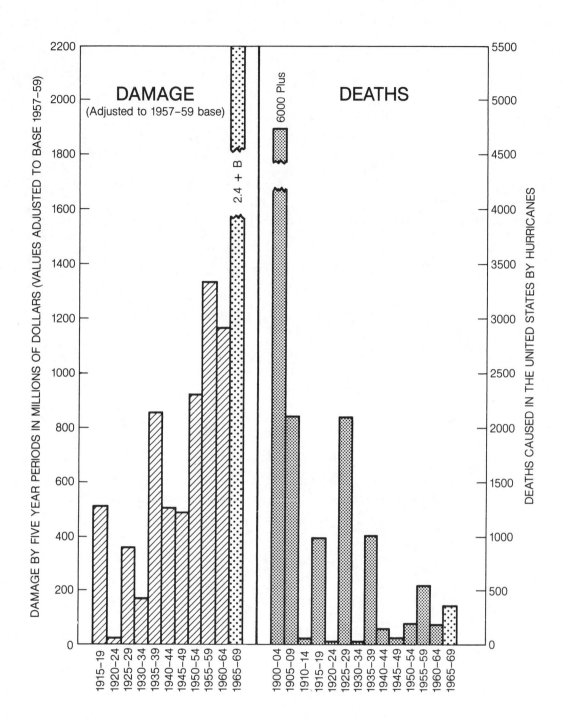

DEATH AND DAMAGES FROM HURRICANES in the United States. Recent years have seen an increase in hurricane damages, and a decrease in deaths caused by hurricanes. (from U.S. Department of Commerce, NOAA, Office of Coastal Zone Management, November 1976. Natural Hazard Management in Coastal Areas)

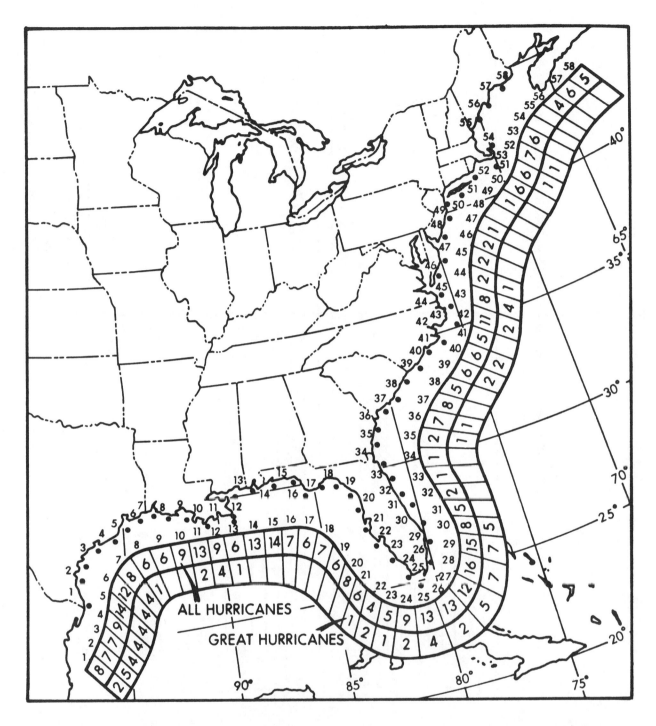

HURRICANE PROBABILITY MAP. The probability (given as a percentage) that a hurricane (winds exceeding 73 miles per hour) or great hurricane (winds in excess of 125 mph) will occur in any one year in a 50 mile segment of the United States Coastline. These probabilities are based on records from 1871 to the present. (from U.S. Department of Commerce, NOAA, Office of Coastal Zone Management, November 1976. Natural Hazard Management in Coastal Areas)

HURRICANE BEACHED FREIGHTERS. Hurricane Camille beached these large freighters at Gulfport, Miss. (Photo by U.S. Coast Guard).

# XI  PORTS

Port facilities are vital facilities for export and import.  Walk to any major port and see the huge amounts of material going in and out--grain from Kansas, coal from West Virginia, oil from Saudi Arabia, iron ore from Venezuela.  Ports also provide many jobs as well as a commercial link, and so public port authorities oversee some aspects of their development.

The U.S. Army Corps of Engineers is responsible for providing and maintaining access to ports.  Since there exist considerable economies of scale in shipping (It is less expensive to ship 1 ton of say coal in a large boat than in a smaller boat) many harbors are being dredged and maintained to greater depths than previously.

# 48. PORT EXPENDITURES—PORT AUTHORITIES

Port development has been funded by both public and private funds. The public funding is typically through local or state port authorities. These quasi-public agencies receive funding through bonds based on municipal collateral, and on collateral based on their own revenue (75%), and from federal, state, and local sources. Their revenue comes from fees charged for port use, and services, as well as rent. The Maritime Administration (part of the Department of Commerce) collects information on public expenditures at 110 ports by survey. These figures indicate that almost five billion dollars have been spent on construction and modernization of pier and wharf facilities in the 33 years preceeding 1979. It is widely believed that private expenditures are equal to or greater than this sum, but specific figures are not available. It is worth noting that the recent trend has been towards the construction of new facilities particularly for bulk and container cargoes rather than towards modernization and rehabilitation of existing facilities. Oil facilities have been privately constructed, and are not reflected here in public expenditures.

Nationally, the port of New York has benefited from more public investment than any other port (over 700 million dollars). Baltimore is second nationally. (1946-1978) On the Gulf coast, New Orleans Louisiana leads with over 180 million dollars in port authority expenditures, and Long Beach, California leads on the Pacific Coast with over 230 million spent by its port authority.

Table 48. PORT DEVELOPMENT EXPENDITURES BY PUBLIC PORT AUTHORITIES (IN THOUSANDS) -- 1946-1978.

| State Port | 1966-1972[2] Total Expenditures | % New | % MR[1] | 1973-1978[2] Total Expenditures | % New | % MR | 1946-1978[3] Total Expenditures |
|---|---|---|---|---|---|---|---|
| Maine | | | | | | | |
|   Portland | 4,048 | 0 | 100 | 1,047 | 64 | 36 | 9,082 |
|   Searsport | - | - | - | - | - | - | 35 |
| New Hampshire | | | | | | | |
|   Portsmouth | - | - | - | 2,298 | 100 | - | 4,706 |
| Massachusetts | | | | | | | |
|   Boston | 69,930 | 92 | 8 | 8,093 | - | 100 | 135,498 |
|   Fall River | - | - | - | 1,756 | 33 | 67 | 3,139 |
| Rhode Island | | | | | | | |
|   Providence | - | - | - | - | - | - | 4,030 |
| Connecticut | | | | | | | |
|   New Haven | 1,692 | 72 | 28 | 6,700 | 83 | 17 | 17,212 |
|   New London | 870 | 0 | 100 | - | - | - | 1,470 |
| New York/New Jersey | | | | | | | |
|   Port of New York & vicinity | 109,516 | 90 | 10 | 110,250 | 96 | 4 | 705,444 |
| Delaware | | | | | | | |
|   Wilmington | | | | 9,168 | 20 | 80 | 25,215 |
| Maryland | | | | | | | |
|   Baltimore | 131,046 | 92 | 8 | 59,715 | 74 | 26 | 274,680 |
|   Cambridge | - | - | - | - | - | - | 1,190 |
| Virginia | | | | | | | |
|   Newport News | 20,900 | 73 | 27 | 1,483 | 81 | 19 | 48,635 |
|   Norfolk | - | - | - | 23,675 | 76 | 24 | 108,129 |
| North Carolina | | | | | | | |
|   Morehead City | 19,473 | 100 | *1 | 10,230 | 100 | 0 | 36,800 |
|   Wilmington | 17,353 | 95 | 5 | 9,352 | 82 | 18 | 40,613 |
| South Carolina | | | | | | | |
|   Charleston | 9,296 | 100 | 0 | 30,750 | 91 | 9 | 66,497 |
|   Georgetown | 1,585 | 100 | 0 | 375 | 100 | 0 | 3,460 |
|   Port Royal | - | - | - | - | - | - | 1,500 |
| Georgia | | | | | | | |
|   Brunswick | - | - | - | - | - | - | 3,047 |
|   Savannah | 19,600 | 100 | 0 | 44,279 | 90 | 10 | 94,526 |
| Florida | | | | | | | |
|   Fort Pierce | - | - | - | 69 | 0 | 100 | 1,789 |
|   Jacksonville | 32,670 | 63 | 37 | 13,730 | 100 | 0 | 54,903 |
|   Miami | 6,910 | 100 | 0 | 13,015 | 98 | 2 | 26,207 |
|   Palm Beach | 535 | 25 | 75 | 7,911 | 93 | 7 | 10,870 |
|   Panama City | 3,139 | 100 | 0 | - | - | - | 3,889 |
|   Pensacola | 2,500 | 100 | 0 | 1,641 | 96 | 4 | 11,141 |
|   Port Canaveral | 1,300 | 100 | 0 | 8,295 | 100 | 0 | 10,825 |
|   Tampa | 47,557 | 96 | 4 | 36,548 | 100 | * | 89,130 |

Table 48. PORT DEVELOPMENT EXPENDITURES BY PUBLIC PORT AUTHORITIES (IN THOUSANDS) -- 1946-1978.

| State Port | 1966-1972[2] Total Expenditures | % New | % MR | 1973-1978[3] Total Expenditures | % New | % MR | 1946-1978[3] Total Expenditures |
|---|---|---|---|---|---|---|---|
| **Alabama** | | | | | | | |
| Mobile | 6,301 | 17 | 83 | 55,192 | 40 | 60 | 95,750 |
| **Mississippi** | | | | | | | |
| Gulfport | - | - | - | 12,252 | 100 | 0 | 18,452 |
| Pascagoula | 10,050 | 71 | 29 | 3,036 | 0 | 100 | 27,111 |
| **Louisiana** | | | | | | | |
| Baton Rouge | 3,170 | 31 | 69 | - | - | - | 46,269 |
| New Orleans | 37,304 | 64 | 36 | 51,852 | 80 | 20 | 187,480 |
| **Texas** | | | | | | | |
| Beaumont | - | - | - | 11,413 | 63 | 37 | 34,708 |
| Corpus Christi | 5,106 | 76 | 24 | 17,106 | 89 | 11 | 61,104 |
| Freeport | 1,215 | 94 | 6 | - | - | - | 6,983 |
| Galveston | 19,400 | 81 | 19 | 40,100 | 90 | 10 | 84,174 |
| Houston | 14,941 | 50 | 50 | 44,774 | 93 | 7 | 116,953 |
| Port Arthur | 13,584 | 100 | *1 | 2,264 | 88 | 12 | 12,010 |
| Port Isabel | - | - | - | - | - | - | 33 |
| **California** | | | | | | | |
| Hueneme | 6,801 | 84 | 16 | - | - | - | 6,899 |
| Humbolt Bay | - | - | - | - | - | - | 560 |
| Long Beach | 41,455 | 51 | 49 | 39,723 | 49 | 51 | 236,197 |
| Los Angeles | 33,424 | 89 | 11 | 36,088 | 86 | 14 | 170,436 |
| Redwood City | - | - | - | - | - | - | 1,694 |
| San Diego | 11,081 | 100 | 0 | - | - | - | 35,864 |
| San Francisco | 32,786 | 56 | 44 | 27,870 | 50 | 50 | 92,510 |
| Ventura | - | - | - | - | - | - | 1,398 |
| **Oregon** | | | | | | | |
| Coos Bay | - | - | - | 9,000 | 44 | 56 | 9,705 |
| Portland | 17,245 | 95 | 5 | 60,600 | 77 | 23 | 105,679 |
| **Washington** | | | | | | | |
| Anacortes | 120 | 100 | 0 | - | - | - | 1,470 |
| Bellingham | 3,238 | 4 | 96 | 400 | 0 | 100 | 6,648 |
| Everett | 3,883 | 91 | 9 | 6,000 | 100 | 0 | 11,543 |
| Gray's Harbor | 9,721 | 97 | 3 | 2,720 | 100 | 0 | 12,823 |
| Olympia | 106 | 0 | 100 | 2,247 | 0 | 100 | 3,650 |
| Port Angeles | 721 | 95 | 5 | - | - | - | 1,101 |
| Seattle | 66,314 | 86 | 14 | 36,947 | 54 | 46 | 136,876 |
| Tacoma | 22,187 | 96 | 4 | 24,000 | 88 | 12 | 53,333 |
| Vancouver | - | - | - | - | - | - | 1,105 |

Sources: * Less than 1%. [1]Modernization and Rehabilitation. [2]Department of Commerce, Maratime Administration March 1974. North American Port Development Expenditure Survey. [3]Department of Commerce, Maratime Administration December 14, 1979. North American Port Development Expenditure Survey (Unpublished Final Draft), provided by Bob Wardwell, MARAD.

# 49. PORT EXPENDITURES—CORPS

The Army Corps of Engineers is responsible for maintaining access to the nation's ports. This requires the expenditures of money--approved project by congress--on navigation projects. The figures presented here are the expenditures made to September 30, 1978.

Paralleling the pattern of expenditures of port authorities, the Port of New York has had the highest construction expense. Along the Gulf coast, Baton Rouge/New Orleans, Louisiana has had the highest construction expense, but on the Pacific Coast, Portland/Vancouver, Oregon and Washington has had the highest construction expense.

Table 49.  EXPENDITURES OF THE CORPS OF ENGINEERS -- NAVIGATION PROJECTS.

| State | Port | Construction | Operation & Maintenance |
|-------|------|-------------|-------------------------|
| ME | Portland | 9,588,710 | 1,915,357 |
| | Searsport | 572,568 | 12,912 |
| NH | Portsmouth | 5,384,043 | 481,859 |
| MA | Boston | 25,313,083 | 6,358,852 |
| | Fall River | 5,550,091 | 1,395,947 |
| CT | New Haven | 4,205,246 | 6,564,471 |
| | New London | 622,994 | 278,034 |
| RI | Providence | 25,417,022 | 3,687,995 |
| NY/NJ | Port of NY & vicinity | 198,761,600 | 104,964,671 |
| DE/PA | Delaware R. | 57,879,028 | 191,964,671 |
| DE | Wilmington | 1,954,725 | 16,792,568 |
| MD | Baltimore | 38,071,275 | 20,783,208 |
| | Cambridge | 195,974 | 53,728 |
| VA | Norfolk/Newport News | 40,665,225 | 40,822,404 |
| NC | Morehead City | 6,527,364 | 16,842,494 |
| | Wilmington | 1,840,958 | 2,575,374 |
| SC | Charleston | 10,037,813 | 53,630,099 |
| | Georgetown | 7,061,755 | 23,489,069 |
| | Port Royal | 1,786,100 | 4,863,540 |
| GA | Brunswick | 4,235,968 | 19,842,149 |
| | Savannah | 42,222,721 | 82,560,940 |
| FL | Fort Pierce | 356,056 | 2,225,915 |
| | Jacksonville | 47,265,962 | 29,480,251 |
| | Miami | 24,412,096 | 2,115,476 |
| | Palm Beach | 6,904,021 | 2,796,616 |
| | Panama City | 1,638,045 | 3,760,538 |
| | Pensacola | 1,469,693 | 3,555,612 |
| | Port Canaveral | 7,341,910 | 11,561,432 |
| | Tampa | 57,704,688 | 10,456,731 |

Table 49.   EXPENDITURES OF THE CORPS OF ENGINEERS -- NAVIGATION PROJECTS
            (cont.)

| State | Port | Construction | Operation & Maintenance |
|-------|------|-------------:|------------------------:|
| AL | Mobile | 15,698,837 | 40,705,964 |
| MS | Gulfport | 904,775 | 18,102,275 |
| | Pascagoula | 6,572,985 | 13,818,331 |
| LA | Baton Rouge/New Orleans | 114,222,690 | 249,534,627 |
| TX | Beaumont/Port Arthur | 56,136,815 | 78,394,758 |
| | Corpus Christi | 38,870,873 | 37,770,855 |
| | Freeport | 2,566,959 | 20,116,667 |
| | Galveston | 29,096,392 | 40,734,104 |
| | Houston | 35,760,382 | 62,003,392 |
| CA | Hueneme | 978,426 | 15,225 |
| | Humbolt Bay | 9,342,509 | 27,932,343 |
| | Los Angeles/Long Beach | 34,896,831 | 3,176,894 |
| | Redwood City | 1,672,722 | 3,452,270 |
| | San Francisco | 2,091,647 | 40,046,543 |
| | San Diego | 26,409,734 | 1,478,264 |
| | Ventura | 1,711,539 | 5,336,584 |
| OR | Coos Bay | 29,193,673 | 31,765,842 |
| OR/WA | Portland/Vancouver | 48,189,597 | 146,292,913 |
| WA | Anacortes | 1,047,607 | 427,886 |
| | Bellingham | 2,570,683 | 62,966 |
| | Everett | 1,775,744 | 3,653,303 |
| | Gray's Harbor | 5,030,851 | 48,867,436 |
| | Olympia | 464,782 | 584,652 |
| | Port Angeles | 470,873 | 47,327 |
| | Seattle | 7,497,942 | 38,151,837 |
| | Tacoma | 2,435,500 | 1,279,534 |

Source:   Adapted from U.S. Army Corps of Engineers, Chief of Engineers.
          FY 1978 Annual Report, Volume II -- Field Reports.

# 50. PORT COMMERCE

Enormous amounts of commerce pass through coastal ports. Incoming oil, and automobiles, and outgoing grain. Many other materials and products pass through these ports. It is worth noting that regionally, the ports with the largest construction expenditure (Table 49) or port authority expense also have the largest reported commerce--New York, New Orleans, Los Angeles, and Long Beach, California.

Table 50. COMMERCE AT SELECTED PORTS -- 1977.

| State | Port | Tons - 2,000 lbs. |
|-------|------|-------------------|
| ME | Portland | 18,326,110 |
|  | Searsport | 1,497,184 |
| NH | Portsmouth | 3,499,854 |
| MA | Boston | 25,975,275 |
|  | Fall River | 5,285,473 |
| CT | New Haven | 11,119,383 |
|  | New London | 3,074,590 |
| RI | Providence | 8,642,484 |
| NY/NJ | Port of New York & vicinity | 185,292,125 |
| DE | Wilmington | 2,917,774 |
| MD | Baltimore | 44,756,359 |
|  | Cambridge | 109,406 |
| VA | Norfolk | 43,862,200 |
|  | Newport News | 8,730,346 |
| NC | Morehead City | 2,904,715 |
|  | Wilmington | 9,504,953 |
| SC | Charleston | 10,629,971 |
|  | Georgetown | 1,798,340 |
|  | Port Royal | 173,488 |
| GA | Brunswick | 1 889,696 |
|  | Savannah | 9,875,678 |
| FL | Fort Pierce | 180,727 |
|  | Jacksonville | 15,108,032 |
|  | Miami | 3,504,543 |
|  | Palm Beach | 681,978 |
|  | Panama City | 1,393,065 |
|  | Pensacola | 3,105,287 |
|  | Port Canaveral | 2,807,463 |
|  | Tampa | 45,619,951 |

Table 50.   COMMERCE AT SELECTED PORTS -- 1977 (cont.).

| State | Port | Tons - 2,000 lbs. |
|-------|------|-------------------|
| AL | Mobile | 35,943,893 |
| MS | Gulfport | 1,094,796 |
| | Pascagoula | 23,832,891 |
| LA | Baton Rouge | 70,008,229 |
| | New Orleans | 162,991,985 |
| TX | Beaumont | 48,918,843 |
| | Port Arthur | 30,753,732 |
| | Corpus Christi | 46,871,695 |
| | Freeport | 15,332,518 |
| | Galveston | 9,563,626 |
| | Houston | 104,291,267 |
| CA | Hueneme | 1,875,743 |
| | Humbolt Bay | 1,644,573 |
| | Los Angeles | 31,325,506 |
| | Long Beach | 32,985,424 |
| | Redwood City | 410,293 |
| | San Francisco | 1,931,693 |
| OR | Coos Bay | 7,599,421 |
| OR/WA | Portland | 21,400,262 |
| | Vancouver | 2,832,673 |
| WA | Anacortes | 8,968,313 |
| | Bellingham | 1,718,417 |
| | Everett | 4,589,002 |
| | Gray's Harbor | 2,646,192 |
| | Olympia | 536,458 |
| | Port Angeles | 3,283,012 |
| | Seattle | 16,432,876 |
| | Tacoma | 10,699,337 |

Source:   U.S. Army Corps of Engineers, Chief of Engineers. FY 1978 Annual
          Report, Volume I--Summary and Highlights, pp. 95-98.

# XII APPENDIX

# 51. COASTAL AREAS

Here, we compare the area of coastal features to one another. This information is summarized from earlier tables. One potentially important classification that is not presented here, nor is it available elsewhere, is the area of nonfederal coastal parks.

The areas in the accompanying figure are shown to be mutually exclusive, but this is not the case. Many acres of wetlands and estuaries are also recorded in other categories such as parks. If we could eliminate the duplication of acreage in several categories, the percentage of uncommited area would increase.

Table 51. COMPARATIVE COASTAL AREAS.

| | Square Miles | Acres | % of Lower 48 | % of Maritime Counties |
|---|---|---|---|---|
| United States | 3,615,123 | 2,313,678,720 | 120.0 | -- |
| Lower 48 | 3,022,261 | 1,934,247,040 | 100.0 | -- |
| Maritime Counties | 182,569 | 116,844,291 | 6.0 | 100.0 |
| Maritime County Farms | 50,039 | 32,025,073 | 1.7 | 27.4 |
| Salt to Brackish Marshes | 7,061 | 4,519,238 | 0.23 | 3.9 |
| Coastal & Tidal Marshes | 13,999 | 8,959,562 | 0.46 | 7.67 |
| Outer Continental Shelf | 875,000 | 560,000,000 | 29.0 | 479.3 |
| Leased OCS | 15,619 | 9,996,196 | 0.517 | 1.78[1] |
| Oil, Gas, Salt & Sulphur Producing OCS | 6,412 | 4,104,086 | 0.212 | 0.733[1] |
| Coastal National Parks | 5,363 | 3,432,418 | 0.177 | 2.9 |
| Coastal National Wildlife Refuges | 1,644 | 1,051,910 | .054 | 0.9 |
| Estuaries | 23,980 | 15,347,000 | 0.793 | 13.1 |

[1] percent of Outer Continental Shelf

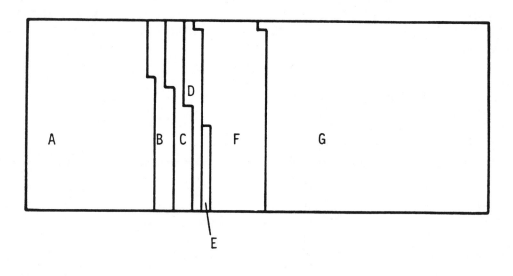

LAND USE IN THE COASTAL COUNTIES.  the large rectangle represents the area of the coastal counties of the lower 48 states (Listed in Table 19).  The subunits within this rectangle represent the area committed to various features as follows:

A.  Farms (Table 20)
B.  Salt to brackish Marshes (Table 29)
C.  Coastal Marshes not in B (Table 29)
D.  Coastal National Parks (Table 41)
E.  Coastal National Wildlife Refuges (Table 42)
F.  Estuaries (Table 26)
G.  Other

Note that many of these features overlap.  That is, there are many acres of marsh within the National Wildlife Refuges, for example.  If we could remove the overlap, the area of G would increase.

# 52. ELEMENTS OF SEAWATER

This table gives some of the elemental components of standard seawater. These elements are in these concentrations the salts in saltwater. <u>Salinity</u>, the concentration of salts in water, comprises 35 parts per thousand in normal seawater. The concentration of salts varies as seawater is diluted by freshwater runoff, especially in estuaries and nearshore waters. The concentration of some of these elements, or the form that the elements take can be altered as a function of biological or industrial processes.

Methodological advances have very recently cast doubt on the concentration of elements which are found in small quantities such as Arsenic, Selenium, and Tin. This is especially true of transition elements, heavy metals, and metalloids. Revisions are currently underway, and should appear in about 1982 in Chemical Oceanography.

Table 52. CONCENTRATION OF CERTAIN ELEMENTS IN SEA WATER.

| Element | Total concentration micrograms per liter of seawater (ppb) | Element | Total concentration micrograms per liter of seawater (ppb) |
|---|---|---|---|
| Hydrogen | 110,000,000 | Gallium | 0.03 |
| Lithium | 180 | Germanium | 0.05 |
| Boron | 4,440 | Arsenic | 3.7 |
| Carbon | 28,000 | Selenium | 0.2 |
| Nitrogen | 150,000 | Bromine | 67,000 |
| Oxygen | 880,000,000 | Krypton | 0.2 |
| Fluorine | 1,300 | Rubidium | 120 |
| Neon | 0.12 | Strontium | 80,000 |
| Sodium | 10,770,000 | Zirconium | 0.03 |
| Magnesium | 1,290,000 | Niobium | 0.01 |
| Aluminum | 2 | Molybdenum | 10 |
| Silicon | 2,000,000 | Silver | 0.04 |
| Phosphorous | 60 | Cadmium | 0.1 |
| Sulfur | 905,000 | Tin | 0.01 |
| Chlorine | 18,800,000 | Antimony | 0.24 |
| Argon | 4.3 | Iodine | 60 |
| Potassium | 380,000 | Xenon | 0.05 |
| Calcium | 412,000 | Cesium | 0.4 |
| Titanium | 1 | Barium | 2 |
| Vanadium | 2.5 | Tungsten | 0.1 |
| Chromium | 0.3 | Gold | 0.004 |
| Manganese | 0.2 | Mercury | 0.03 |
| Iron | 2 | Thallium | 0.01 |
| Cobalt | 0.05 | Lead | 0.03 |
| Nickel | 1.7 | Bismuth | 0.02 |
| Copper | 0.5 | Thorium | 0.01 |
| Zinc | 4.9 | Uranium | 3.2 |

Source: Peter G. Brewer, 1975. Minor elements in seawater <u>In</u> J.P. Riley and G. Skirrow [eds.] Chemical Oceanography Volume <u>I</u> 2d edition.

# 53. CONVERSION FACTORS

Conversion factors for common units are presented in these tables. The units across the top of the table are the starting units, and the units in the column on the left are the final units. The body of the table is the factor by which the starting unit is multiplied to obtain the final product. For example, how many square miles are there in 1,000 acres? From Table 50b. multiply 1,000 by 1/640 and find that 1,000 acres is 1.56 square miles. Conversion of metric units is simply a matter of moving decimal points as the unit prefixes change. For example, 59 centimeters is 0.59 meters.

Table 53a. LENGTH CONVERSION FACTORS.

| | Centimeter | Inch | Foot | Yard | Meter | Kilometer | Mile |
|---|---|---|---|---|---|---|---|
| Cm. | 1* | 2.54* | 30.48* | 91.44* | 100* | $10^5$ | $1.609 \times 10^5$ |
| In. | 0.394 | 1* | 12* | 36* | 39.37 | $3.973 \times 10^4$ | 63,360* |
| Ft. | $3.28 \times 10^{-2}$ | 1/12 | 1* | 3* | 3.281 | $3.28 \times 10^3$ | 5,280* |
| Yd. | $1.094 \times 10^{-2}$ | 1/12 | 1/12 | 1* | 1.094 | $1.094 \times 10^3$ | 1,760* |
| Meter | 0.01* | $2.54 \times 10^{-2}$* | 0.305 | 0.914 | 1* | 1,000* | $1.609 \times 10^3$ |
| Km. | $1 \times 10^{-5}$* | $2.54 \times 10^{-5}$* | $3.05 \times 10^{-4}$ | $9.14 \times 10^{-4}$ | $1 \times 10^{-3}$ | 1* | 1.609 |
| Mi. | $6.214 \times 10^{-6}$ | 1/12 | 1/12 | 1/12 | $6.214 \times 10^{-4}$ | $6.214 \times 10^{-1}$ | 1* |

Table 53b. AREA CONVERSION FACTORS.

| | $Ft^2$ | $Yd^2$ | Acres | Hectares | $Km^2$ | $Mi^2$ |
|---|---|---|---|---|---|---|
| Sq.ft. | 1* | 9* | 43,560* | $1.076 \times 10^{-5}$ | $1.076 \times 10^7$ | $2,788 \times 10^7$ |
| Sq.yds. | 1/12 | 1* | 4,840* | $1.196 \times 10^4$ | $1.196 \times 10^6$ | $3.098 \times 10^6$ |
| Acres | $2.296 \times 10^{-5}$ | $2.066 \times 10^{-4}$ | 1* | 2.471 | 247.105 | 640* |
| Hectares | $9.297 \times 10^{-6}$ | $8.361 \times 10^{-5}$ | 0.4047 | 1* | 100* | 258.999 |
| Sq.km. | $9.297 \times 10^{-8}$ | $8.361 \times 10^{-7}$ | $4.047 \times 10^{-3}$ | 0.01* | 1* | 2,590 |
| Sq.mi. | $3.589 \times 10^{-8}$ | $3.228 \times 10^{-7}$ | 1/12 | $3.86 \times 10^{-3}$ | 0.386 | 1* |

Table 53c.  VOLUME CONVERSION FACTORS.

|            | Liter          | Gallon (U.S.)  | Cubic Foot | Barrel (oil) |
|------------|----------------|----------------|------------|--------------|
| Liter      | 1*             | 3.785          | 28.316     | 158.987      |
| Gallon     | $2.642 \times 10^{-1}$ | 1*     | 7.481      | 42*          |
| Cubic foot | $3.532 \times 10^{-2}$ | $1.337 \times 10^{-1}$ | 1* | 5.682 |
| Barrel(oil)| $6.290 \times 10^{-3}$ | $2.381 \times 10^{-2}$ | 0.1777 | 1* |

Table 53d.  MASS CONVERSION FACTORS.

|           | Gm.            | Lbs.           | Kg.            | Short Tn.      | Metric Tn. |
|-----------|----------------|----------------|----------------|----------------|------------|
| Gm        | 1*             | 453.6          | 1,000*         | $9.070 \times 10^5$ | $10^6$* |
| Lbs       | $2.205 \times 10^3$ | 1*        | 2.205          | 2,000*         | $2.205 \times 10^3$ |
| Kg        | $10^{-3}$*     | 0.4535         | 1*             | $9.070 \times 10^2$ | 1,000* |
| Short Tn. | $1.103 \times 10^{-6}$ | $5 \times 10^{-4}$ | $1.103 \times 10^{-3}$ | 1* | 1.102 |
| Metric Tn.| $1 \times 10^{-6}$* | $4.536 \times 10^{-4}$ | $1 \times 10^{-3}$ | $9.070 \times 10^{-1}$ | 1* |

Table 53e.  HYDROCARBON WEIGHT AND ENERGY EQUIVALENTS

<u>Weight equivalents</u>
1 Barrel of Crude Oil (Domestic) = 295 pounds (42 gallons)
1 Barrel of Gasoline = 259 pounds (42 gallons)
1 Barrel of Liquified Petroleum Gas = 190 pounds (42 gallons)

<u>Energy equivalents</u>
1 Barrel of Crude Petroleum has the energy value of 5604 cu. ft. of
   Natural Gas-Dry
1 Barrel of Crude Petroleum has the energy value of 0.228 short tons of
   Anthracite Coal
1 Short Ton of Anthracite Coal has the energy value of 4.379 barrels of
   Crude Petroleum
1 Short Ton of Anthracite Coal has the energy value of 24,541 cu. ft. of
   Natural Gas-Dry
1 Barrel of Gasoline has the energy value of 0.90 barrels of Crude Petroleum
1 Barrel of Gasoline has the energy value of 5070 cu. ft. of Natural Gas-Dry
1000 cu. ft. of Natural Gas-Dry has the energy value of 0.178 barrels of
   Crude Petroleum
1000 cu. ft. of Natural Gas-Dry has the energy value of 0.041 short tons of
   Anthracite Coal

---

* Exactly
Source:  ASTM-IP Petroleum Measurement Tables

Table 53f.  METRIC PREFIXES.

| Prefix | Factor by which unit is multiplied |
|--------|-----------------------------------|
| giga   | $10^9$      |
| mega   | $10^6$      |
| kilo   | $10^3$      |
| hecto  | $10^2$      |
| deka   | $10$        |
| deci   | $10^{-1}$   |
| centi  | $10^{-2}$   |
| milli  | $10^{-3}$   |
| micro  | $10^{-6}$   |
| nano   | $10^{-9}$   |
| pico   | $10^{-12}$  |

# 54. STATE RANKS

How do the states compare in their coastal characteristics?  This table ranks the states in 17 important categories.  Louisiana ranks first most often.  It leads in the percentage of the shoreline undeveloped, the area of estuaries, the area of wetlands, and the weight of the 1978 fisheries catch.  In all cases, the states are ranked from highest (1) to lowest (21).  The letters at the head of each column are interpreted below.

| Column | Ranked Based on | From Table |
|--------|-----------------|------------|
| A | Length of general coastline | 1 |
| B | Length of tidal shoreline | 1 |
| C | Percentage of privately owned shoreline | 2 |
| D | Percentage of undeveloped shoreline | 3 |
| E | Percentage of shoreline as beaches | 4 |
| F | Percentage of noneroding shoreline | 5 |
| G | Percentage of general shoreline length fronted by barrier islands | 8 |
| H | Percentage of coastal county area in farms | 20 |
| I | Percentage of population in coastal counties | 21f |
| J | Percentage of electrical generating capacity in coastal counties | 22 |
| K | Area of estuaries | 25 |
| L | Area of coastal wetlands | 28 |
| M | Area of Coastal National Wildlife Refuges | 42a |
| N | Weight of the 1978 fisheries catch | 34 |
| O | Value of the 1978 fisheries catch | 34 |
| P | Weight of the 1978 fisheries catch per fisherman | 36 |
| Q | Value of the 1978 fisheries catch per fisherman | 36 |

---

footnotes

* ties are ranked according to the average rank that the states would receive if they were not tied.  Thus, for example if three states are tied for the first rank, they would all be ranked second.

Table 54.  STATE RANKS

STATE RANK IN CATEGORY:

State

| | A | B | C | D | E | F | G | H |
|---|---|---|---|---|---|---|---|---|
| Maine | 7 | 3 | 1 | 11 | 20 | 20 | -- | 18 |
| New Hampshire | 20 | 21 | 14 | 20* | 4 | 16 | -- | 13.5* |
| Massachusetts | 8 | 14 | 9 | 17 | 2 | 17 | 13 | 15 |
| Rhode Island | 17 | 18 | 6 | 20* | 6 | 19 | -- | 17 |
| Connecticut | 21 | 16 | 8 | 20* | 7 | 18 | -- | 13.5* |
| New York | 12 | 12 | 16 | 16 | 8 | 21 | 6 | 21 |
| New Jersey | 11 | 13 | 17 | 14 | 10 | 11 | 5 | 11 |
| Delaware | 19 | 19 | 12 | 8 | 14 | 6 | 11 | 2 |
| Maryland | 18 | 8 | 4 | 18 | 21 | 15 | 1 | 4 |
| Virginia | 13 | 7 | 10 | 7 | 15 | 12 | 8 | 6 |
| North Carolina | 5 | 5 | 20 | 4 | 13 | 8 | 2 | 8 |
| South Carolina | 9 | 10 | 21 | 5 | 19 | 2 | 9 | 7 |
| Georgia | 14 | 11 | 11 | 2 | 9 | 5 | 4 | 19 |
| Florida | 1 | 1 | 5 | 9 | 17 | 4 | 10 | 5 |
| Alabama | 15 | 17 | 2 | 13 | 3 | 9 | 3 | 9 |
| Mississippi | 16 | 20 | 15 | 12 | 12 | 10 | -- | 16 |
| Louisiana | 3 | 2 | 13 | 1 | 11 | 13 | 12 | 10 |
| Texas | 4 | 6 | 7 | 6 | 18 | 3 | 7 | 1 |
| California | 2 | 4 | 18 | 10 | 16 | 14 | -- | 3 |
| Oregon | 6 | 15 | 19 | 15 | 5 | 7 | -- | 12 |
| Washington | 10 | 9 | 3 | 3 | 1 | 1 | -- | 20 |

Table 54. STATE RANKS

STATE RANK IN CATEGORY:

| State | I | J | K | L | M | N | O | P | Q |
|-------|-----|------|----|----|-------|----|----|----|----|
| Maine | 11 | 5 | 19 | 16 | 8 | 7 | 7 | 17 | 18 |
| New Hampshire | 16 | 12 | 21 | 20 | 20.5* | 21 | 20 | 18 | 17 |
| Massachusetts | 10 | 9 | 14 | 13 | 14 | 5 | 3 | 7 | 3 |
| Rhode Island | 1.5* | 1.5* | 17 | 21 | 18 | 13 | 15 | 8 | 8 |
| Connecticut | 6 | 3 | 20 | 17 | 19 | 19 | 19 | 20 | 20 |
| New York | 8 | 10 | 12 | 14 | 17 | 15 | 13 | 21 | 19 |
| New Jersey | 9 | 7 | 7 | 6 | 6 | 9 | 10 | 5 | 9 |
| Delaware | 1.5* | 1.5* | 11 | 11 | 9 | 20 | 21 | 10 | 16 |
| Maryland | 7 | 6 | 4 | 9 | 11 | 14 | 14 | 19 | 21 |
| Virginia | 13 | 13 | 3 | 7 | 10 | 3 | 8 | 3 | 15 |
| North Carolina | 20 | 17 | 2 | 8 | 4 | 6 | 11 | 4 | 14 |
| South Carolina | 17 | 16 | 10 | 4 | 5 | 17 | 17 | 15 | 5 |
| Georgia | 21 | 21 | 16 | 5 | 7 | 18 | 18 | 16 | 10 |
| Florida | 4 | 4 | 6 | 2 | 1 | 8 | 5 | 12 | 11 |
| Alabama | 19 | 19.5* | 9 | 15 | 20.5* | 16 | 12 | 11 | 2 |
| Mississippi | 18 | 14 | 13 | 12 | 16 | 4 | 16 | 1 | 4 |
| Louisiana | 12 | 11 | 1 | 1 | 2 | 1 | 2 | 2 | 6 |
| Texas | 14 | 15 | 5 | 3 | 3 | 12 | 4 | 13 | 1 |
| California | 3 | 8 | 8 | 10 | 12 | 2 | 1 | 6 | 7 |
| Oregon | 15 | 19.5* | 18 | 19 | 15 | 11 | 9 | 9 | 12 |
| Washington | 5 | 18 | 15 | 18 | 13 | 10 | 6 | 14 | 13 |

167

# INDEX

169

Shellfish (cont.)
    bioconcentration factors, 39
    biocontamination, 41
    endangered, 124
Shoreline
    length, 5
        general coastline, 5
        national shoreline, 5
        tidal shoreline, 5
    ownership, 6
        federal, 6
        nonfederal public, 6
        private, 6
    uses, 7
        nonrecreational, 7
        recreational, 7
        undeveloped, 7
Swimming, see recreation
Temperature
    change in nuclear power plants, 74
    conversion factors, 34
    sea surface, 34-35
Threatened species, 114-124, 132
    defined, 114
Tide
    causes, 30
    patterns, 30-31
    ranges, 31-33
U.S. Army Corps of Engineers
    erosion control expenditures, 11
    port expenditures, 154-155
    role in dredge and fill permits, 90-92
U.S. Coast Guard
    role in reporting oil spills, 45
U.S. Department of the Interior
    endangered species, 114
    oil and gas leases, 75
Water
    freshwater flow, 24-27
    quality, 36-52
    sea water elements, 161
    use by nuclear power plants, 73
Water Pollution Control Act, 45
Water Skiing, see recreation

Wetlands
    area
        most recent estimates, 84,88
Wetlands
        original, 84
        1780, 84
        1954, 84,87
    dredge and fill permits, 90-92
    loss, 84
    types
        area (1954), 84,87
        defined, 85
    wildlife use
        by state, 94
        by wetland type, 93
Weight
    see fisheries, energy,
    conversion factors
Whales, see mammals
Wildlife
    in wetlands, 93-94
    refuges (see Audubon Society;
        estuaries, sanctuaries;
        National Parks, National
        Wildlife Refuges, The Nature
        Conservancy)